Holy Man, Holy War

by

Fred Berry, Jr.

Published by:
Emerald Ink Publishing
7141 Office City Drive
Suite 220
Houston, Texas 77087

(713) 643-9945
Fax (713) 643-1986
E-mail emerald@emeraldink.com
http://www.emeraldink.com

Printed and bound in the United States of America

Library of Congress Cataloging-in-Publication Data

Berry, Fred, 1936-
  Holy man, holy war / by Fred Berry, Jr.
  p. cm.
  Includes bibliographical references.
  ISBN 1-885373-10-4
  1. Jesus Christ—Rationalistic interpretations 2. Jesus
Christ—Political and social views. 3. Bible stories,
English—N.T. Gospels. 4. Palestine—History—To 70
A.D. 5. Insurgency—Palestine I. Title.
  BT304.95.B47 1997
  232.90151dc21

Table of Contents

About the Author

The author, Fred Berry, Jr., Retired USAF Lieutenant Colonel, served seventeen years in counter-insurgency with Air Commandos, now called Special Air Warfare (their specialty —assault airlift for Special Forces). He received a B.A. in Economics from the University of Arkansas, and his M.A. in Historical Studies from the University of Houston at Clear Lake.

Raised in a fundamentalist atmosphere, Fred studied the Bible and tried to fill in the blanks in the Scripture. He heard a member of the Christian Coalition announce the details of their plan to take over the government. "I could care less what people believe as long as they don't make laws to force me to conform to those beliefs," he reacted. Then he wrote this book, which will add to the one already in the Library of Congress, *Counterinsurgency: Kennedy's War in Viet Nam*.

He studied the life of Jesus Messiah from all of the mountains of surviving texts and modern academic studies. He wove them into a feasible and plausible narrative biography of Jesus, but primarily as an insurgent, *with notes and references to support the observations and conclusions.* **The resulting portrait clashes with current popular concepts.**

Introduction

Sixty thousand books have already been written about the life of Jesus Messiah. At any one time at least 100 books concerning Jesus are in print. All this material, every page, every thought of every author, every smear of ink, every illustration of every creative artist, is tainted with prejudice and motive. It doesn't take long for a perceptive reader to note an author's objective. This author is no exception.

In recent years, a flurry of scholarly theses attempted to uncover the 'historical Jesus.' These works often represent years of research and thought. However, they too often present a common problem in readability. They are scholarly books by academics for academics. Academics advance narrow hypotheses tested page after page increasingly. To one who would read for pleasure, the endless arguments presented to test and prove one small bit of evidence have a quick and sure sedative effect. Too often the academic's prejudice and motives exude so much mumbo-jumbo that the reader accepts the flimsiest theory out of sheer exhaustion.

Diametric to the supposed appeals to reason and logic of the academic is the manipulation of the reader to preconceived notions—*argumentum ad hominem*—by narrowly centered Biblicists. No matter how loosely based on carefully selected portions of only one source of evidence—the Bible—'reverential reconstruction' of the life of Jesus, by definition, shuts out all attempts to reason and logic. The reader is told what he wants to hear in a pleasant, upbeat narrative. Selected portions of the Bible are often referenced by either annotation or inference. The motive is to promote the author's prejudice. The prejudice is unreasoned faith.

Reverential reconstructions, written or verbal, are harmless when they only reinforce the readers' or listeners' superstitions. My concern is that these thought training devices affect far more people than the willing individual reader. Believers are motivated to actualize their concept of a perfect society upon those of us who have other ideals. They use political processes and, when that doesn't work, force of arms.

Devotees of the reverent reconstructionists are uninhibited in their zeal to remake my psyche in their image. It is truly amazing to me—unindoctrinated me—how these modern day zealots can refer to the teaching of Jesus when they try to enact laws and develop powerful cultural mores. They would:

- prohibit abortion,
- force school children to repeat prayers,
- outlaw the consumption of wine,
- limit drug use to that approved by the State,
- force what they call 'family values,'
- make the punishment of a crime be based on the motive and not the injury, and
- encourage more production and less reasoning by creating more material want.

These things might or might not be desirable for society as determined by human reason, but to claim they are derived from the teaching of Jesus is ludicrous. As the reader shall see, Jesus taught just the opposite. It is very wrong for a modern political conspiracy to claim otherwise.

I believe Jesus the man was much more than either the academics or the fundamentalists see. He was the teacher of a philosophy of life that cannot be followed by a person within modern society. He was a master of illusion. He used the power of faith to heal. He led a terrorist insurgency to establish God's rule on earth. He was even deified by his followers after his death.

Certainly, it is very difficult to read much that was written about Jesus by the ancients without noticing the obvious contradictions, distortions and purposeful lies, but those are for the Biblicists to deny and the academic historians to sort out in their quest for the historical Jesus. My aim is less ambitious and more fun than either. My hope is to present an interesting, coherent, readable story of the life of Jesus. In order to maintain the continuity demanded of a biography, I was forced to discard much contradictory material, retaining that which made sense in the telling of the life of a person, however mythologized or unbelievable might be the tales that were written about him. Readability demanded more weight be put on one aspect of the life of Jesus. I present a theme not a thesis. I, too, have a motive. My motive is to identify the insurgent role of Jesus.

Religious warfare and terrorism did not begin or end with Jesus. The horrors of wars to establish the good and right are very much with us today. Antagonistic teaching such as that of Jesus is not well received in today's society. Modern govern-

iv

ments are not prone to accept armed groups fanatically anticipating an imminent God sanctioned overthrow of that government. Religious fanaticism that extends to politics is not too long tolerated in today's cultures unless the government itself is irrational. The story of Jesus is one of fanatical religion-based politics not tolerated by Rome. It is not the benign philosophy of Paul.

Jesus' role in insurgency has been glossed over and ignored by Biblicists and only briefly mentioned by most academics. I clearly see an insurgency described in the synoptic gospels and the book of John. Even though it would have been very dangerous to have been too specific about personal involvement in sedition against Rome during the time *Matthew, Mark, Luke* and *John* were written, much evidence of insurgent activity should, nevertheless, be apparent to the reader of those books and other gospels of that period.

The reality of Jesus began to be changed even before his death. He was a hope, a thread of hope for a people who had been politically subjugated and culturally attacked for at least one hundred years by the Romans and by other powerful neighbors many times during their well recorded history. Rumor spread that this teacher, healer, philosopher, and fury revolutionary would be the savior of their culture. If he were to be king, he, by definition, was a son of God just as were King David and King Solomon before him. The capture and quick execution of Jesus extinguished all hope he was to be the new king and savior of the Jewish nation.

The writings of former intimates of Jesus—or their first generation students—had to apologize for the death of Jesus and failure of the insurgency. A myth that Jesus was still alive was formulated, but time brought doubt. By the time Matthew, Mark, and Luke began to write what became to be known as the synoptic gospels, the reality was that Jesus was a semi-God, carried up into a heaven somewhere above the earth to await a *time within the readers lifetime* to return to rekindle the insurgency. That never happened. The synoptic gospels were changed somewhat during the lifetime of their writers to reflect reality. Later, these texts were further altered by copyists' mistakes and design.

Even while the first writers were still alive, the Jewish nation became, strangely enough, an object of detestation by the followers of Jesus. The longed for Kingdom of David was to be hated, not saved. The Romans became good and noble by all accounts after they humiliated and destroyed the Jewish population just before the synoptic stories and the gospel of John were to be written.

The slanting of the gospels of the disciples to reflect the reality of the period following the Roman destruction of Judea and Israel does not eliminate their value as source material to my story. Myths appeal to the deepest emotions of a people, not to truth based on reason. For that reason, I have attempted to discard the emotion of that moment and find the fascinating fable of a man who actually lived, breathed, and fought for what he thought was right.

One aspect of the religion that has become loosely known as Christianity for which I can little compensate is its astonishing ability to change and re-interpret what has been recorded in the past. **Today's Christianity in no way resembles what was taught by Jesus.** It is not what was written by the ancients. However, even considering the problems of language translations, deliberate changes, 'modernizing' meaning and spelling, changing syntax, and the viewing of history from the perspective of another time, a fascinating story jumps out of the gospels at the reader who would, as Jesus might have said, "read with his eyes open." I hope the reader of this book will note my references without prejudice.

Three hundred years after the death of Jesus, Emperor Constantine of the Byzantine Empire made Christianity essentially the State religion. The government of Byzantine was extremely bureaucratic. Just about every aspect of commerce and daily life was codified and tracked. The religion of Christianity was no exception. Constantine assembled what he considered the most correct and wisest teachers of Christianity in the Empire. This group is known as the Council of Constantinople of 381, C.E.

From a mountain of written material purported to be true and God blessed by one group or another, the Council selected some 152 works to be the officially sanctioned Word of God. These texts were not presented in their present English language form until 1611 as the Authorized or King James Version of the Holy Bible. Until the recent rise of modern democratic institutions, other written work concerning the life and philosophy of Jesus was suppressed. Religious leaders, firmly backed by self-righteous governments, often condemned to death any person found to possess any religious material not approved by the Council of Constantinople.

We are fortunate that much forbidden material survives. A group of gospels collectively called *The Lost Books of the Bible*, apocryphal gospels, was first assembled and published in 1926. Scholars generally accept the premise that these texts were written in the same time frame as the New Testament, but argue the motives and veracity of the authors. I find the stories no more or less believable than those found in the texts selected by the Council of Constantinople. I use these texts without prejudice for the purpose of telling the story of Jesus as it was recorded.

The Lost Books fill a huge gap in the life and personality of the young Jesus that is completely missing from approved texts. I trust most readers of the Lost Books quickly discover why those authorities charged to maintain fixed notions of the State Religion of Christianity during the time of Constantine might have feared them. The story of young Jesus did not fit paganized Pauline ideas of what he should have been. The mere fact that these books have been so viciously attacked by religious leaders raises their status in my reckoning.

The apocryphal gospels I utilize to help tell the story of Jesus are attributed to Matthew, James, Thomas, Nicodemus, Pontius Pilate and Peter. These authors are no more or less authenticated than those of the New Testament.

One text that might have been missed and therefore not approved by the Council is The Gospel of Thomas. It is a compilation of statements attributed to Jesus by his brother, Thomas the Twin. I have found it most useful as it indicates Jesus was very involved in insurgent activities. The Gospel of Thomas was part of the Nag Hammadi library rediscovered in 1945. It is likely the most authentic of all gospels as it was translated directly from original documents by unprejudiced linguists.

I have also adopted parts of many scholarly theories and theses in as much as each enhances my limited objective to present a coherent biography. I was particular interested in English translations of the Dead Sea Scrolls and comments concerning their significance by those who have devoted much of their lives to understanding these historical treasures. I give credit to all authors listed in the bibliography for any background study that might have helped me gain some insight into the life of Jesus. However, except as noted, I have not purposefully adopted any specific theory to defend or deny.

In spite of the voluminous material available concerning the life of Jesus, small gaps and insufficiently explained incidents remain. In order to effect my objective to present an interesting, coherent and readable biography, I have filled those gaps with whatever insight I may have gained from the study of Jesus and war and insurgency. Call these additions theory if you wish. I hope they make sense and add continuity to the story.

From the motive and prejudice of ancient authors and modern historians I have attempted to find a logical chronology of an incredible life. I hope those who are secure in their faith— whatever it might include—will read this account as a fascinating fable. Others—without any particular prejudice—should realize that the stories of Jesus are myths passed on to explain, protect and enhance cultural values. The military tactician and others trained in counter-insurgency will, no doubt, understand the difficulties inherent in overcoming an insurrection led by a popular holy teacher such as Jesus.

This composition attempts to relate the story of how one man, holy and righteous, claimed divine sanction for an insurgent war to overturn an unpopular government and tried to establish a rule of God. The kingdom that he would have had rise out of the ashes of insurgent war would last forever. Its first ruler would have been Jesus, the spiritual leader of the insurgency.

As evidenced by the first four books of the New Testament and other sources, Jesus spoke of three distinct kingdoms. One was the Kingdom of the House of David (God), which Jesus was sent to rule. The second was the Kingdom of Spirit that lives within each of us. The last was the Kingdom of Heaven.

The Kingdom on this earth that Jesus intended to rule was imminent, real and very material. He spoke of it often in those gospels that purport to record his words. Those who fought for the Kingdom would reap vast rewards. Jesus even promised that those who died in the cause of his insurgency would live forever in a better land. That promise is chillingly echoed in today's holy wars.

The kingdom that Jesus promised to those who would die for the earthly kingdom of God was within the psyche of each person. That spirit would live forever within the essence of being that remains after bodily death. This concept, a common thread in many religious doctrines, is often lost to many of those who call themselves Christians. So many parables and so much teaching of Jesus tells us the Kingdom is a feeling within each of us. It is truly amazing when people believe that they can in death escape their own essence to be transported to a wonderful world of nothingness called Heaven.

Jesus taught that the place—and it was a place—called the Kingdom of Heaven was not for humans, quick or dead. "And no man hath ascended up to Heaven, but that he came down from Heaven, even the Son of Man which is in Heaven" (John 3:13). Abraham ruled Heaven (John 8:39 and Luke 16:19-31). Heaven was filled with saints who were apparent sub-gods such as Moses, Isaac and Jacob. These sub-gods made at least one appearance on earth as if human. Angels in Heaven also possessed God-like powers. "There was war in Heaven..." (Revelations 12:7). There was much violence (Matthew 11:12). Heaven was not perpetual as was the spirit of man. "Heaven and earth shall pass away, but my words shall not pass away" (Matthew 24:35 and Mark 13:31).

The reader should note that the kingdom addressed in this book, unless otherwise made clear, is that of this material earth. I do not mean to minimize the humanism of much of the teaching and some of the deeds of Jesus as reported by his disciples. However, I do find his teachings fragmented, inconsistent and contradictory as recorded. This perception may be in the recorders' fault or it might be my inability to find more in the text than is written.

The story of Jesus is classic tragedy: a mortal man seeking what is good and noble is overcome by the contradictions within himself.

The Kingdom of God on this earth did not materialize. The tragic failure is told in the word of the ancients. Listen and you shall hear.

Mother of Jesus

"And you shall recount in the book the story of Mary:
how she left her people and betook herself to a solitary
place to the east."

The Koran, "Mary" 19:12.

Disgusting in its habits and ugly to the unappreciative, yet a most prized possession in ancient times, the camel shaped history as did no other single animal. Not until 1100 years before the common era[1] was this strange looking animal domesticated to the point of carrying men and products long distances across inhospitable terrain. By the time of the reign of David and Solomon in Israel over one hundred years later, the camel had linked cultures, eased the hardships of life by opening trade routes, and increased man's range of knowledge. The evolution of the ability to inscribe communicable thoughts and econmic data on portable materials made the transfer of knowledge possible.[2]

The sailing ship did for coastal regions what the camel did for the landlocked. Sails capable of a broad reach opened societies to trade and cognitive intercourse. Interchange of ideas and products accelerated both economic and intellectual development of sailing peoples. Merchants and traders within sailing societies tended to benefit in a more concrete way. They often became very wealthy in earthly terms.[3]

The coastal region just north of Samaria and Judea—the land of Asher—benefitted from both the advent of the sail and the domestication of the camel. As the beginning of the common era neared, the region around Sepphoris and Nazarene was a crossroads of trade and commerce. Most caravan traffic from the ports of Ptolemais, Tyre, and Sidon passed through that region en route to Samaria and Judea. Virtually all commerce from the Jerusalem area to Damascus and Mesopotamia utilized one of the two roads through Nazarene.

The Asher tribe of Tyre and Galilee was among the most worldly and knowledgeable people of Biblical times. They became rich merchants and traders as their ships and caravans visited all the known world. While other sons of Abraham became so obsessed with religion that their talents little benefitted the community, the Ashers developed their abilities fully. Their artisans and carpenters were so technologically advanced that Solomon was forced to hire them to design and build the grand Temple and Palace at Jerusalem instead of local Israelites.[4] Their understanding of nature and life, borrowed from Greek, Egyptian, Assyrian, and eastern societies, clearly exceeded those groups nearer Jerusalem. It was from this heterogenous culture that Jesus Messiah, religious teacher, philosopher, lawmaker, physician, magician, and militant leader of a revolution, inherited much of his character.

A man called Asher, father of the Asher tribe, was born of a slave called Zilpah about two thousand years before the Messiah. Zilpah was maidservant to Leah and Jacob. Leah picked Zilpah to conceive her husband Jacob's children after the first surrogate mother, also a slave, proved unable to produce more than one son. Others 'maidens' were impregnated by Jacob in the rather eclectic family. Leah, the wife, did conceive Jacob's last two children, but only after she discovered the therapeutic properties of the personal narcotic used by her sister Rachel's son.[5]

Asher's brother, Judah, was the progenitor of Joseph, husband of Holy Mary.[6] Asher was the progenitor of Mary through her mother, Anna.[7] Both the House of Asher and the House of Judah were blessed to be ruling royalty.[8] Neither was poor. Records show that heads of each clan lead armies for the conquest of Canaan and for the defense of their war-won domain.[9] About seventy-eight generations passed between Asher and Judah and the mother and father of Jesus.

The land of Asher as established after the twelve tribes' successful conquest of Canaan (about 1200 BC) never fully integrated into the empire of David and Solomon. Instead, its interests were linked to its neighbor to the north, that seagoing people that was Phoenicia.

Periodically, the kings of Israel attempted to consolidate Asher into greater Israel and Judea, but Asher resisted close association with the less progressive House of David. Asher seemed more interested in the profits of trade and commerce than in the many wars the greater Kingdom launched. One specific incident is recorded. King Hezekiah forced the clan leaders of Asher to humble themselves before him and to attend Passover in Jerusalem every year. Hezekiah considered the Asher tribe to be 'divers,' those who took divergent approaches to the worship of the single God, YHWH.[10]

As the beginning of the common era approached, any unity of those supposed sons of Abraham that had been the twelve tribes was more pretended than real. The area encompassing the long deceased Kingdom of David and Solomon was not only under Roman military rule but also split along religious, ethnic, economic, and cultural lines. There was much hope that a new king, a Messiah, would arise out of the lineage of David. Certainly, there was no shortage of religious and underground political leaders ready to bring that hope to fruition.

The sect that seemed most certain the New Kingdom was at hand was the Essenes. The Essenes numbered about 4,000 living throughout the former kingdom of David. They were led by about three hundred priests centered in a remote monastery called Qumran. About fifteen years before the common era, they activated a plan they hoped would produce a leader to overthrow the present government and replace it with a new God-ruled Kingdom of David. The principle instrument of their scheme was a married couple of some wealth and position and of the proper lineage with a deep belief in the Essene faith. From that couple a female would be born that would be trained from infancy to be the mother of the Savior of the Kingdom. Her story is told in myth.[11]

The parents of Holy Mary, mother of Jesus, were Anna and Joachim. Neither lived in Tyre at the time of their betrothal. Anna's family was of Bethlehem and claimed to be aristocratic descendants of King David even while her pedigree branched to the tribe of Asher. Joachim was of the land of Galilee and claimed the priestly dynastic succession from Aaron. His wealth helped make him a leader of the community, but worship of the single God dominated his daily life.

Joachim and Anna remained childless for twenty years after marriage. During that painful time, they piously worshipped the single God and obeyed every religious law known to them. They lived plain and unpretentious lives. Joachim's considerable income was divided into three parts: one-third was given to the Temple and priests of their sect, one-third Joachim and Anna distributed among the poor, and the remainder they retained for themselves and their family. Thus, they lived in faithful devotion to their God and fellow man, but they could not produce the one thing that would make them happy—a child. They so wanted a child that they promised God they would surrender it to the monastery for the service of Him if He would so bless them.

In the twentieth year of their marriage, Joachim returned from the Passover feast in Jerusalem heavy-hearted. There were tears in his eyes when he spoke to his aging wife, "I am not worthy. I have sinned, yet I know not how. I have seen thirty-six winters. Thirty-six times the shepherds have driven their flocks down from the pastures. Thirty-six times they have returned to the green spring grass of the mountains. Still, God has not blessed me with that which I most desire, a child."

Anna touched him on his shoulder. It was the knowing touch of loving familiarity. "God knows," she lied. "As he has favored you with worldly wealth, so shall he bless you with a child. Your seed shall be preserved and the world will rejoice. Have faith. Perseverance will prevail."

"Issachar, the High Priest, reproached me." Joachim continued as if he had not heard his wife. "He blamed our childless condition upon my lack of earnest compliance to the will of God. Why should he say that? Why?"

"He is but a Sadducee. He shall be denied the resurrection. He is nothing more than a puppet of the great puppet."[12]

"But, he is the High Priest. We are children of Israel. We must surely respect the High Priest."

"No. We follow the Righteous Teacher. He shows us the true way. Why do you fear that which is of this earth?"

"My friends were there," Joachim's thoughts again wandered. "My brothers, whom I love greatly, were there. Many of our tribe were there when he ostracized me—when he cut the tie that binds us to our heritage."

"He is a fool, a dupe of Rome." Anna felt fear at such utterances, words that could condemn her to death by stoning.

Joachim seemed not to hear. He spoke in a near whisper, barely audible to Anna standing by his chair. "He refused my offering. He said I was not worthy to appear among those who had given Israel sons. I will always remember his judgment! He said, 'Cursed is everyone who shall not beget a male in Israel!' He decreed that only after I proved free of this curse of sterility, when I did beget a son, would he welcome my gifts into the service of God."

Anna knew the great shame and pain her husband felt. He had not returned home from the pilgrimage with his neighbors; instead, he had gone alone to his pastures. There he had remained with his servants, the tenders of the herd, for several days. Anna's heart ached but she could do little to relieve the hurt of public reproach.

Joachim sought the grace of God through another avenue. He bypassed the Temple and attempted to contact God directly. He did not return to a public place. Instead, he followed the tradition of Moses and went alone into the desert for forty days and forty nights of fasting, prayer and meditation. While he was there, a spirit visited his thoughts and the Holy Ghost impregnated Anna.

Joachim, without food or drink, alone in the hot desert sun and cold dark nights, reached fatigue. In a state of somnolence where reality blurred into fantasy, an angel visited him.

The angel spoke, "Fear me not, dear Joachim. I am sent by God to tell you your prayers will be answered. God has delayed giving you a child so that when she is born, she shall be a gift of God and not a product of lust. Have you not studied the births of many ancient fathers of Israel who were born of women thought to be barren? Sarah gave life to Isaac in her eightieth year. Rachel and Jacob conceived Joseph, the founder of the House of David, only after many years of marriage. And were not Samson, the great judge, and Samuel, the blessed prophet, born of women who had been dismissed as barren? So too shall you and Anna be blessed.

The angel continued with an astounding revelation. "Anna, your wife, shall bring forth a a daughter and you shall name her Mary. Mary shall be filled with the Holy Ghost even before birth. You must, according to your vow to God, give her to the Temple while she is yet a baby. There, in the Holy of Holies, she will from infancy be made ready to be mother of the Messiah. She shall see no evil. She shall know nothing of the common people who are often coarse and filled with worldly desires. She shall neither touch nor eat anything that is unclean. As Mary reaches womanhood, she shall give virginal birth to Messiah Jesus, and Jesus shall be the saviour of all the tribes of Israel." The angel commanded Joachim to go to the Golden Gate of Temple Jerusalem. There he would meet Anna who would surely rejoice to see him.

The angel departed and Joachim wondered.

As Joachim made his way from the desert to the Golden Gate, the angel paid another surprise visit. It appeared before Anna in the seclusion of the beautiful Joachim home garden.

Joachim had not told Anna that he was going into the desert to do penance. She was very worried. She thought herself a childless widow and cried, "I will mourn for both my widowhood and my barrenness."

Anna wore the black hood of mourning. Her handmaid, Judith, reminded her, "It is the time of the feast. Is it not unlawful for a believer to mourn?"

Anna bristled. "Leave me," she shouted. "I will not allow a slave to speak with such a lack of respect. Perhaps it is you who cast this evil spell upon me. Here, take this hood that you also may be cursed."

Judith refused the hood. She answered calmly, "What evil can I bring you when you will not listen to me? It is your God who has cursed and closed your womb!"

Anna vexed in contemplation. She put on her best garment and walked into the garden to pray. There, she prayed to God that she, like Sarah before her, would give birth after menopause. She noticed a bird's nest with little blind chicks crying with mouths open for their mother. "Am I not like these birds, oh Lord? Even the beasts of the earth are fruitful. I am less than brute animals, fishes of the sea, or even worms in barnyard manure, for they reproduce their kind according to your plan. Oh, God, help me to find my place as a fulfilled woman!"

Anna, on her knees, bowed her head and closed her eyes. She slowly began to feel a warm glow near her. As she looked up, the glow brightened and changed into the form of an angel.

The angel spoke, "Anna, your prayers are heard. You will conceive and bring into this world a progeny who will be known to all mankind, and you shall call her Mary."

Anna answered. She repeated her vow that the baby, male or female, would be dedicated to God. The angel told Anna to go to the Golden Gate of the Temple. There, as a sign from God, she would find Joachim joyfully awaiting her.

As the angel spoke to Anna, Joachim was traveling to the Golden Gate. He felt full of joy and the grace of God. As he passed his slaves tending to his large estate, he shouted to them, "Bring me ten perfect she-lambs. They shall be a gift to my God upon the Temple altar. And select twelve calves for the priests. Oh, yes. Bring a hundred goats for the common people."

As Joachim's entourage of servants and animals approached the Temple gate, he beheld the glowing face of his wife. He jumped from his high camel perch and ran to her. She threw open her arms and they embraced fervently. "I know that I am blessed by God. I thought that you were dead and that I was a widow. I thought I was barren but I am now with child. The single God of Abraham heard our prayers."

The couple and their slaves returned home to Galilee. After one day of rest at home, Joachim ventured to the local temple. The temple priest wore a special God-appointed instrument as headwear, a crown with a brightly polished dome. It covered much of the forehead. The faithful would look into the polished ball. If the reflection they saw was clear, it meant that they were free of sin. If the reflection faded deep into the dome, it meant that they were doomed. Joachim saw a bright, clear image of himself.

Eight months later, Anna gave birth to a a beautiful girl child. She was named Mary.

Anna and Joachim took extraordinary steps to keep Mary clean and holy until she was weaned of breast and surrendered to the priests. Mary's infancy conformed to every known law and religious tenet, She was from the moment of birth raised as if she were the bride of God. There was constant prayer in Mary's presence. The baby Mary's chamber became a holy place. Normal human baby inquisitiveness was discouraged. Mary was to be a perfect vassal of God.

When Mary took her first steps at nine months of age, Anna felt frightened. She forced Mary to stay in a pen with a ceiling so low that she could not stand upright. Only undefiled virgins were allowed near the baby.

On the occasion of Mary's first birthday, the priests of the monastery of Qumran[13] visited her and made arrangements to have her delivered to them when Anna was no longer able to give suck. The priests reminded the parents that the infant was promised to God.

At age two, Mary was ready to be delivered to the monastery, but Anna and Joachim held onto her for almost one more year. As Mary approached three years of age, Anna and Joachim could no longer delay the fulfillment of their vow. They made ready for the painful journey.

Seven virgin princesses with lighted lamps led the way to the monastery. Late at night, they arrived at the foot of the twelve flights of stairs that led to the monastery temple doors. Joachim and Anna disrobed to cleanse themselves as required by law and custom before ascending the stairs with Mary. To their amazement, the baby Mary stood upright and straight away ran up the steep stairs to the waiting priests. The aging Anna and Joachim would never see their blessed child again.

Mary was raised in the monastery with other prospective mothers of the Messiah. She was by far the brightest, most beautiful and most insightful as to the ways of God. It seemed that from age four, Mary understood her future role. From that young age, she tried to prepare herself for her place in history. She studied the Torah and the teachings of the Essene sect. She absorbed the prophecies of the expected coming of the new King of Israel, especially. She learned to read and write the idiom of her father. She studied Greek, Aramaic and the language of the pharaohs. She felt at home with her God within the dark walls of the place of learning. She excelled in the study of magic. The teacher within the monastery told her of the slavery of the Jewish populace she could not see. She sensed the excitement of the glory days of King David eight hundred years before. Her every essence told her that she would be central to the return of that kingdom. As the virgin within the monastery came of age, it was apparent that Mary was to be selected as mother of the king. One test remained.

As the other young candidates left the monastery to seek earthly husbands, Mary did not go. She was escorted to Temple Jerusalem for the final test. A great curtain for the main altar had been woven with great love and care. All that remained to complete it to the satisfaction of God was for it to be dyed the True Purple of the Royal House of David. The test was for Mary to produce that color that only God could make.

Mary did not hesitate. She asked for certain ingredients and she heated water in huge vats within the hall. The final result was a deep, regal blue-purple that was even more striking than the famous Tyrolean purple. The priests were exhilarated. Mary had proven that she was anointed by God.

She went back to the monastery at Qumran. Now the only female in that cold place, she refused to return to the community, citing her vow to remain chaste. What had to be done to create the Messiah would have to begin in the monastery.

Soon, the same angel, Gabriel, that had visited her mother appeared in the faint evening light within Mary's bedchamber. Gabriel told her that she would conceive by the Holy Ghost and give virginal birth to the King. He commanded her to call the child Jesus.

On another night, the Holy Ghost visited Mary in the form of a man. The seed of God was planted.[14]

The priests at Qumran hoped Mary might be pregnant.

Zacharias, the High Priest of Qumran and an uncle of Mary, did not speak for days. When he did, it was with great wisdom. "Call together the sons of David. We shall select an old widower who shall be husband of Mary. Mary shall give virginal birth to the King of Israel. Long live the King. Long live Israel."

Joseph

*"Therefore the Lord himself shall give you a sign;
behold, a virgin shall conceive, and bear a son, and shall
call his name Immanuel."*
The Holy Bible, "Isaiah" 7:14.

A sense of excitement and urgency soon filled the monastery. That month, Mary did not bleed.

The priests of Temple Qumran sent out word that all widowed and divorced males who were direct descendants of David should come to the temple to be interviewed. The one man who proved himself worthy would become the husband of the mother of the New Kingdom.[1]

The priests had a well-defined standard in mind for the successful candidate. He would first and foremost be a direct descendent of David. This also required that he be of a recognized princely family, a family known within the community as an economic and cultural leader. A poor family would have much to overcome to win acceptance as the genitors of the husband of the woman who was to give birth to the King. Then, as now, a prince seemed more likely to be the father of a king than would a commoner.

Related to the requirement that the husband be of a princely family was the need to find someone who would provide material comforts to Mary. Mary's well-to-do parents were not alive. Her uncle Zacharias loved her very deeply and was concerned for her physical as well as her spiritual well-being. The priests also understood that a wealthy husband would be more likely to provide a healthy environment for the baby king.

Because Mary was well-educated, her earthly husband would ideally be a well-educated and refined man of the world. He would be a well-traveled yet pious person. These traits would add to his status as supposed father of the King.

The last qualification for the husband/keeper of Mary was that he be of advanced years. The priests sought someone who had already experienced love and fatherhood, someone who had proven himself willing and capable of loving and caring for children. This called for an older widowed man or one who had been divorced for a good and lawful cause. The husband of Mary would accept the condition that he was to be the caretaker of a virgin.

All these qualities, and more, would be embodied in a man who came to be known as Joseph.[2] Joseph not only possessed the qualities of royal lineage, economic position, age, and marital status, but he also carried a deep hate for the Herod clan. Salomé, the daughter of King Herod the Great, forced him to divorce his first wife and bear the humiliation and pain of knowing his wife was a sex slave for Salomé's benefit.

Joseph waited outside the chamber where seven Essene priests interrogated prospects, one by one. Fifty sons of David milled around the open, barren yard awaiting an audience with the seven who could bestow immortality upon their name. All were supposedly related through forty generations of King David's blood. Joseph knew many, but not all of them. He identified as much with Egypt as he did with Israel. He began to wonder why he had been so arrogant as to suppose he might be selected as the husband of the holy mother.

As a servant signalled, each candidate entered the one tall, narrow door into a long, high, otherwise featureless stone hall. A period of ten to fifteen minutes elapsed before each candidate re-emerged through the door, head bowed, silent and expressionless. The cycle would then be repeated.

Time dragged on. There was no conversation, no outward excitement within the group awaiting interrogation, only the sound of an occasional belch and grunt from a camel in the nearby stables. Water gently flowed from a large cistern through a low viaduct that intercepted the east side of the yard.

The sun sank low into the western sky, Joseph found himself alone. All other candidates had taken their turn, entered the lonely door and returned silently to make their way across the yard and down a perilous path cut in the rock cliff toward the river Wadi Qumran.

Joseph sat on the ground, head cupped in his hands and knees. He didn't hear the servant glide up behind him.

The servant tapped Joseph on the shoulder. Joseph looked up. He thought the servant must be deaf and dumb. The servant pointed at the door, indicating Joseph was expected within the chamber. Joseph was filled with fear. He shook his head in fearful dissent, but the stern face of the servant was insistent. Joseph arose and warily made his way toward the foreboding door. A powerful spirit entering his body—a sense that he was to inherit a central place in history—almost overwhelmed him. He timidly entered the opening.

The dimly lighted chamber at first hid its features from Joseph. The bright sunlight had constricted his pupils. Slowly, his eyes adjusted to the darkness. Slightly elevated dining cots lined each long wall. The room was only about twenty feet across, but fully sixty feet long. A wide aisle down the center of the room separated the dining areas. A light from the far end of the hall illuminated another entrance that led to the central courtyard of the complex. At the far end by the courtyard portal sat the seven priests at a long table.

"Welcome, Son of God," the center priest beckoned Joseph forward.[3] Joseph recognized the Head Priest as Zacharias, keeper of Mary.

"You are a Son of David?"

"I come," Joseph began as he groped down the aisle toward the council. "I come.... I come unworthy to be the husband of Holy Mary!"

"Who tells you so? Is it not we who shall judge? Are you filled with the Devil?"

"No. No," cried Joseph as he fell to his knees. "I have tried to be righteous. I have obeyed the will of the single God of Abraham and followed the ways of the Righteous Teacher, but I am old. I have seen too much. My body is weary. My years betray me."

"We shall judge!"

"Are you rich?"

"Is your table blessed with abundance from God?"

"Herod has stripped me of princely authority. I have only four camels, fifty sheep, a small herd of goats and ten asses. But my vineyard is blessed, my home is happy and my slaves are contented."

"What are your talents?" inquired one priest. "How do you help light the world?"

"Some call me a carpenter," Joseph carefully answered. "I trade with caravans from Tyre for fine wood from which I make precious jewelry boxes and fine furniture. I sometimes help build houses in the land of the great river."

"Then you know of the products from both Tyre and the distant east, do you not?" the priest at the dark end of the table asked with a knowing grin.

Joseph would not be trapped. "Yes, I know of the drugs. I know the bitter wine of death. I know that which burns the sick fumes of darkness, but I do not deal in such things," he caustically defended himself.

"Are you Egyptian? To whom do you profess loyalty?" Zacharias asked, changing the focus of questions, but maintaining the pressure. Zacharias knew full well every aspect of the life of Joseph.

"My father was of Israel and Judea. Although I reside in Galilee, I am a Son of Abraham. I serve only the God of David."

"Do you believe the return of the Kingdom of David is near?"

"I believe the Messiah is near. I shall see the New Kingdom in my lifetime."

"Then you are a Zealot?"[4]

"Some have said so, but I am not. I know the Kingdom will be established by God. We mere men need not, and should not, attempt to control the will of God. The Kingdom of God is by God and not man. Mortal man need not attempt to hurry the coming."

"You have known the gods of Egypt. To whom do you pray?"

"To the God of David.I know no other."

"You have credentials?"

"I have the rod of my ancestors.It is my dearest possession."[5]

The family rod was the most precious possession of an adult male within the twelve tribes.The rod was a long cylindrical container which held a tightly rolled Parchment scroll. Upon this scroll was the complete family genealogical tree of its subject owner. It was proof of a male's tribal rights as well as his legal place in Jewish history. A most treasured and likely most dangerously incriminating rod in the days of the Herod impostors was one that indicated a direct claim to the true monarch lineage of King David, the root of David's father, Jesse.[6]

Joseph carefully laid his rod before the Head Priest, Zacharias. The priests appeared stunned when they noticed the covering that protected the cylinder. The cylinder was adorned with a tightly woven material of the most beautiful deep purple color. The priests knew it was the *True Purple*.

The True Purple could be worn only by those of the royal House of David.[7] The secret formula for True Purple could only known by sanction of the single God. The priests had seen True Purple only once before, but now as then, they understood its significance. The True Purple's deep, rich, radiant color could not be matched by an unanointed person anywhere in the world known to the priests.

The True Purple was, of course, from the same secret formula that Holy Mary mixed for the great Temple curtain. It was an undeniable sign that Joseph was God-anointed to be the husband of Holy Mary.

If the priests needed more to persuade them who should be the husband of Mary, they would not have long to wait.

The head interrogator reached for the rod lying on the table in front of him. To his surprise, a snow white dove suddenly appeared perched on the rod. When the priests reached to touch it, the dove flew away, through the door, into the sky until it could no longer be seen by human eyes.[8]

The priests were convinced. The dove fulfilled a prophesy that would announce the coming of the Messiah.

"You are Joseph," Zacharias pronounced."Yours shall be a hallowed place in history, You may leave."

Joseph picked up his rod and turned to walk back down the long aisle to the exit door.

"No," Zacharias corrected him. "Leave through this door to the central courtyard. There you will find servants to help you prepare for the ceremonial dinner. You shall be the guest of honor, husband of Mary."

The next morning, in the same chamber hall, Zacharias conducted the betrothal proceedings. Joseph saw Mary, his promised one, for the first time. The couple repeated the pledges. Zacharias reminded Joseph that betrothal did not sanction sexual intercourse. "You must care for this one and treat her as you would your own child. Her chastity is essential to fulfill the prophesies."

Joseph well understood. He had read the word of Isaiah. He knew the virgin birth of the Messiah and the horrible war with Assyria that would explode around his coming.[9] He thought, "This is a strange place to begin the process that will take so many lives and cause so much pain," but he would accept his duty to be husband of the virgin.

That afternoon, shortly after the betrothal. Joseph and Mary mounted camels for the trip north to Joseph's house in Galilee. Mary's birthplace was very near her new home. Mary and Joseph spent the first night in the home of Essene believers in Jericho. They then followed the well-marked road near the

River Jordan northward. The second night, they slept under the stars on the banks of the river near the temple Zaphon.At the town of Seythopolis, they rested for the third night. The last day, they departed early, entered Galilee, the Tetrachy of Herod Antipas. On the fourth day they arrived at the small, dusty village that was to be known as Nazareth. In all, they had traveled seventy miles in four days.

Mary's reputation as future mother of the New Kingdom of David preceded her to Galilee. When she presented some True Purple dye to the local high priest, he declared her blessed for all generations to come.When Elizabeth, the young wife of the aging Zacharias and cousin of Mary, answered Mary's knock at the door, she blessed Mary as mother of the Lord. Even the unborn baby inside Elizabeth leapt and blessed Holy Mary.

Joseph could find little demand for his carpenter talents in the small farming settlement. He now had six children and Mary to care for. His modest herds and vineyard simply would not provide for his responsibilities. That pitiful dowry would hardly feed the servants so Joseph sadly decided to return to Egypt to work. As soon as he insured Holy Mary's comfort in her new surroundings, he departed by camel. Mary remained behind to act as surrogate mother and manage the estate.

Soon after Joseph left, Mary began to feel the baby inside her body. She was afraid and hid herself from the streets. She wore long, loose robes when near the children. She was fourteen.

As Joseph journeyed home, he became anxious. He felt something strange was occurring in Nazareth. Entering his house, he found Mary large with child. He was very disturbed. Joseph felt he had not honored his pledge to the Priests of Qumran and to Israel. He had left the virgin Mary alone to be seduced. He cried, "Is not the history of Adam repeated in me? For, in the very instant of his glory, the serpent came and found eve alone and seduced her."

Joseph did not understand how Mary, educated in the "Holy of Holies," nourished by angels and groomed as a saint, could have sold her soul for a few moments of pleasure.

Rumors spread throughout the community that the virgin Mary was pregnant. Speculation was that the father was a man from distant Gaul named Pantera.[10] Pantera was a young Roman soldier that Mary welcomed into her house when his group encamped nearby. Those rumors persisted for centuries, but they were not true. Mary was pregnant before she left the monastery with Joseph.

"As the Lord of God lives, I know not by what means I have become pregnant," she protested. "I have known no man."

But, Mary remembered the angel's visit to the dark chamber in the monastery.

Joseph was only betrothed to Mary. Aside from his promise to the Qumran priests, betrothal did not give the right for sexual intercourse between couples. It was akin to a sexless trial marriage. Betrothal was a promise to love and care for each other. Only after the trial period was the marriage consummated by the act of sexual intercourse between a betrothed couple. Considering Mary's condition, Joseph was understandably suspected of having had sex with her, thus marrying her in secret.

Joseph was afraid that he might be condemned for breaking his vow to the priests or that Mary might be convicted of adultery. He did not wish to see this young woman stoned to death. He had grown fond of her strange angelic beauty. He believed Mary's story that the expectant father was an angel of the Lord.

There was one option that Joseph could employ to be rid of the predicament in which he found himself. He could accuse Mary of unfaithfulness and proclaim three times, "I divorce you." This would exonerate Joseph and condemn Mary to death. His growing love for Mary made that option unpalatable.

While Joseph pondered his problem, the Holy Ghost visited him in his sleep. The Holy Ghost declared that he, the Holy Ghost, was the father of the child. He told Joseph to proudly accept the gift that Mary was to bring to him and the people of Israel. He was told to name the child Jesus Immanuel.[11] Jesus would be the savior of Israel and the king of the Kingdom of David. Joseph remembered Isaiah.[12]

The story of the immaculate conception would not go unchallenged. It would soon be tested in the court of the God of Abraham.

When the troubled Joseph did not make an appearance outside his home after his return from Egypt, a local transcriber of documents named Annas became worried and visited the home Joseph and Mary. There he noticed Mary was pregnant. He angrily accused Joseph of breaking his vow by secretly marrying Mary.

Mary and Joseph denied any misconduct but their story of Holy Conception was not acceptable to Annas. He brought charges against Joseph before the High Priest of Galilee. The High Priest was aware of the Essene scheme and saw a trial as a perfect opportunity for God to demonstrate the truth of Mary's virgin impregnation and vindicate Isaiah's prophesy.

The High Priest held court near the village water well. "You are accused of blasphemy against God and willfully breaking your holy covenant with the priests of Qumran. How do you respond to those charges?"

Joseph humbly bowed his head, "It is the will of God. Only He may judge."

"So it shall be," the Priest/judge seemed to retort. "God will test your guilt or innocence. You shall drink the poison water and retire to the mountain. If after three days you live, that will prove you are guiltless and Mary's condition is indeed supernatural. If you die, Mary must return to the monastery where she shall surely be stoned to death. God will decide."

The poison was a product of Tyre.[13] Its secret ingredient was imported by sailing vessel from the Greek city of Cyrene in what was to become North Africa. In addition to being the base for True Purple dye, when mixed with alcoholic wine-vinegar and mandrake it made an aberration—a depressant that slowed the heartbeat to the point of apparent death. A whole healthy person could tolerate measured doses of the potion. With a frail, sick, or injured recipient, however, a dose too large could cause death. The priest gave Joseph only enough to simulate dying.

Joseph drank the poison, turned and walked slowly toward a nearby mountain. He slumped to the ground in the shade of a large rock only about two hundred yards from the water well. There he was soon overcome by deep sleep. One or two villagers approached him, then reported to the priest that he was dead. The priest proclaimed, "It is written: the test must consume three days. Leave him untouched until the third day."

Annas was overjoyed but his joy did not last long.

On the third day, after two nights, Joseph appeared at the water well, alive and healthy. God had saved him, some said returned him from the dead. His innocence was no longer in doubt. Most important, the prophesy of Isaiah would now be realized. Mary would give virgin birth. It is said all Israel rejoiced.

The High Priest, likely quite knowledgeable of the earthy source of Mary's condition, neatly set the.stage for the fulfillment of the prophesied virgin birth of the Messiah King. An abiding faith in an early appearance of the Messiah who would be King of the New Kingdom was the cement of Essene behavior, but the urgency of that faith being actualized was enhanced greatly by very earthly dealings.

Because of the belief in an imminent coming of the Messiah, when time would somehow be frozen, the Essenes living within the community at large did not feel the same compulsion to raise large families as did other Jews. As a growing number of Essene men and women felt an overpowering need to devote their lives to God, the urge to procreate was subordinated.[14] Because the average age of the sect membership grew older, it became more difficult to recruit new young members. "Followers of the Book" became older and more fixed in their beliefs. They knew that righteous and pious devotion would assure each a place in the New Kingdom within their lifetimes.

The Essene priests helped the prophesies of the coming Messiah along a bit. Mary, born of Essene parents and educated in the Temple as a saint, was to give birth to the new King of Israel and Judea. Of that, the priest made certain.

One problem remained. The new king was to be of Bethlehem, the land of David. Mary lived in Galilee.

Mary became large with child. The Coming was near.

Birth and Infancy

*"He relates that Jesus spake even when he was in the
cradle and said to his mother, 'Mary, I am Jesus the Son of
God, that word which thou didst bring for according to the
declaration of the angel Gabriel to thee, and my father hath
sent me for the salvation of the world.'"*

Lost Books of the Bible, "Infancy of Jesus," 1:2-3.

In the fourth year after the death of Herod the Great in the reign of Caesar Augustus, the Herod clan, claiming God-given dynastic right, ruled administratively all of Roman-controlled Israel, Judea, and Galilee. The first son of Herod the Great, Herod Archelaus, was Governor/ King of Judea. His brother, Herod Antipas, ruled Galilee by decree with the help of Roman troops. Salomé, their beautiful and sulky sister, enjoyed a lordship of her own.

Tradition and culture of the Israelite peoples demanded a God-ordained king figure as the glue to hold together diverse tribal societies. They also demanded that the King function as a persuasive religious leader to codify superstitious notions and define acceptable interpersonal behavior. At the beginning of Jewish history, these two functions resided in a single person. Abraham founded a belief system based upon a singular divine entity and ruled his small tribe with a firm hand by sanction of the divinity. As his tribal family grew, it became more difficult for one person to be all powerful. Hundreds of years after Abraham the Israelites were divided into twelve tribes, Moses still managed to be both the religious and cultural leader. During the reigns of David and Solomon, the functions began to divide into two offices: the kingship and the priestly order. It was essential in the minds of the people that each office be anointed by God. Naturally, an aristocratic lineage evolved as God tended to anoint close friends and family to ascend to each office as it became vacant. Popular dissatisfaction with the existing power structure by those on the outside, such as the Essenes, created concepts of a savior/ruler who would re-establish a powerful God-centered Kingdom. A valiant attempt to bring that concept to fruition followed.

The Herod family was not accepted as a God-sanctioned authority by the Israelite people. Israel and Judea were like a high rock wall with no binding mortar. Tension permeated this society. People felt that the faintest wind could bring the wall crumbling to the ground.

Mainly as a result of the diminished acceptance of the monarchy, the priestly hierarchy also suffered declining influence. The traditional government of the Israelite people had actually become a two-pronged theocracy. On the one side was the God-sanctioned, yet secular, kingship. The king ruled supreme in external matters. His charge was to deal with foreign governments in a manner worthy of the Jewish people. He had complete power to raise armies, fight wars and conquer territory. He dealt with tribute and collected taxes to maintain the royal house. The King's physical presence served as a symbol of pride and unity among the Israelites. He gave them a sense of kinship that approached nationalism.

The other half of the dual government, the religious hierarchy, developed as a more direct conduit from God to the people. Priestly authorities did much more than attend to the people's metaphysical needs. In addition to religious teaching, the priestly population interpreted and enforced written law handed down by Moses and other sages. The direct instruments of law enforcement were the local councils and the central council called Sanhedrin. Priests also foretold events in a manner calculated to increase religious reverence and promote patriotic unity. They controlled a paramilitary police force. Much of the formal educational process of all young boys and rich young girls was conceived and administered by priests. The finest and most costly physical structures were built in support of the priestly establishment. Priests healed by driving out demons and identifying persons who were possessed by evil spirits. The large priestly organization was supported by not so voluntary tithing. The influence of the huge priestly authority organization permeated every segment of Jewish society and Israeli economics at the beginning of the common era. It had a much greater impact on daily life than did the kingship.

During the Herod dynasty, a third force affected the life of every citizen—Roman military presence. Roman interests in Israel and Judea did not extend beyond maintaining peace among various traditional rivalries in order to promote trade and commerce of Mother Rome. For the maintenance of the military presence and the peace it insured, Roman procurators recruited local Jews to collect taxes and tribute. While this created some conflict between Rome and the ruling priests, Rome—for the most part—maintained a low profile by limiting appearances of Roman troops outside their enclave around Caesarea.

It was the priestly authorities who ran the everyday government that touched the lives of every citizen. It was they, directed and guided by the single god YHWH, who judged and dealt justice in all matters concerning misbehavior such as theft, murder, usury, adultery, and blasphemy. When God failed to bring lawbreakers to trial, the large Temple police organization could always be relied upon to supplement Its will. The priestly authorities also handled all civil disputes. Roman military officers judged and punished only those accused of crimes directly against the interests of the Roman Empire: treason, insurrection, failure to pay taxes to Caesar.

This three-sided government was under attack at the beginning of the new era as reckoned by the new calendar. Clearly, the populace felt alienated from all three. A very historic people, a people whose religion approached ancestor worship, had lost their sense of historical continuity. Whether actually severe or limited, the wrongs committed by government authorities were perceived as grievous.

Active opposition to government slowly materialized. Israelites found it difficult to comprehend that the traditional protectors of their welfare and heritage had become dupes to a strange foreign power. Opposing established institutions such as the priesthood and the kingship was painful. Nevertheless, numerous deviant religious sects mixed with covert political insurgencies to attempt change.

A vacuum of government seemed to exist within a fragile glass container surrounded by a growing mass of societal pressure. The shell appeared so thin that a child might break it. Two babies of the royal House of David did crack it beyond repair; one was John the Baptist who attacked the very foundation of the religious structure and the other was anointed to be King and prophet.

In an area of southern Galilee which came to be known as Nazareth,[1] two young princesses carried developing revolutionaries within their wombs. They feared an uncertain future.

"We are blessed, my dear cousin," Elizabeth counseled Mary. "Although our husbands are old and do not lie with us, the Holy Ghost has planted the seeds of life within our bellies. We must be thankful we are able to help perpetuate the nation of Israel and extend the pedigree of the royal House of David. Do not cry."[2]

"But I fear Herod the great usurper will surely learn of our royal progeny. He will seek them out and kill them. We must hide."

"God will protect us," Elizabeth answered Mary. "God is the father, the genitor of our children. He will allow no harm to befall them."

"Herod Archelaus has summoned all from the House of David to gather in Bethlehem to be counted. Why should he want all those who could possibly prove true descent from King David? When the revolution comes—and it will come—the Messiah shall arise from the ranks of the Davidians and he shall be king of the true, the great and the righteous kingdom of the Israeli people."

Mary remembered the words of the angel in the night, "And your child shall be called Jesus." She felt the child jump within her body.

"Augustus...," Elizabeth began to speak, but thought better of it.

"I know," Mary continued the sentence. "Caesar Augustus published the order, but it is Herod that most fears us Davidians. This census will help Herod remain in power. Herod will know who to watch. Power begets power. Evil power begets evil."

Stunned, Elizabeth arose to bide Mary farewell. "I shall go to Qumran. There I will meet Zacharias, my husband. Perhaps we will see you and Joseph in Bethlehem for the census. Bless you, Daughter of God." They embraced.

Joseph prepared to make the trip to Bethlehem. The children would remain at home under the care of house servants. He worried for Mary who was in her eighth month of pregnancy. Since she was not an accomplished camel rider, the high perch might prove too dangerous to chance. A horse drawn cart was impractical for the route planned. He consulted the local priest about how to honor his vow to protect and care for Mary and still comply with the census edict. The priest advised him that since he alone was responsible for the young virgin, he must take her with him to Bethlehem.

Joseph called for a donkey to be prepared for the journey. The donkey made an appropriate tribute to the unborn messiah. The donkey, a symbol of the working poor with which the approaching insurgents could identify, a lowly beast of burden, remained strong and stubbornly persistent when it felt its rights threatened. The donkey, sure-footed and hardy, did not seek the smooth, well-traveled path. This frail-looking animal could carry heavy loads for long distances. The burdens of the coming fight could be long, cumbrous and dangerous. The poor were ready.

The summons to Bethlehem neatly served the purposes of the planned insurgency. It was essential to acceptance by the Israelite faithful that the Messiah be born in Bethlehem as they had been told so many times the prophets Isaiah and Ezekiel had prophesied. If those who feared the Davidic dynasty had intended harm by the census, they greatly miscalculated. The Messiah would now be born in Bethlehem! The prophecy that the Messiah would be born in the city of David would now be fulfilled. If the call to Bethlehem had not occurred, it would have had to be invented.[3]

Joseph and Mary departed southern Galilee for Bethlehem in early fall. Other Davidians joined them along the improved rock road to Jericho. The procession was at first solemn, heads bowed, looking at sandaled feet being warily placed one in front of the other. But, as the warming sun climbed higher overhead, the mood of the crowd changed to joyful expectation.

A very old man walking alone, tapping his staff on the rock road in quick solid jabs, began to reflect aloud. The travelers eased closer to hear him. His was a message of hope. "....the House of David. The Holy shrine to our revered ancestors. We shall meet to celebrate the birth of the new King—David reincarnated. The Kingdom is at hand. The usurpers, the evil priests, the strange invaders from the north, shall as it was prophesied by Isaiah be destroyed and driven from the promised land of God. The Messiah is here with us. He shall lead this nation to renewed glory and we shall prosper in the eyes of the Lord Messiah forever and ever."[4]

Mary smiled and felt the baby inside her body. It was as if God were speaking through the old man.

The old man's glad tidings quickly spread throughout the southward-bound procession. As the word passed from traveler to traveler, it was embellished to the point of predicting a miracle. The new Messiah became not just a king, but also an incarnation of God itself. The Messiah would be more than Lord over the nation. He would be the Lord-God upon this earth and in heaven. He would possess everlasting life and give everlasting life to all who worshipped. His arrival would be announced by a convergence of stars such as the world had never seen — a huge fireball of stars hanging in juxtaposition over the birthplace of the Messiah to guide all the Jewish to him.[5]

News of the coming king arrived at the royal castle of Herod well ahead of the first Davidians from Galilee. Herod knew the scriptures. He had studied the ancient writings and psalms that foretold of a Davidian Messiah. He feared that those scriptures would be used to gain support for an insurgency and brooded over how best to contain the situation.

In Jericho, Joseph and Mary separated themselves from non-Essene Davidian travelers. They rested in the same home they had enjoyed during their recent betrothal trip northward. Mary retired to their inn-like quarters early for a much needed rest. Joseph conversed with his hosts long into the night on matters of religion and politics. The next morning they set out southward for Qumran. The path became rough and treacherous. The hardy donkey proved his worth as Joseph led it, Mary carefully balanced atop its swayed back, over and around obstacle after obstacle.

At Qumran, they rested for the evening before turning west. By this little-traveled route, they could not only enjoy a visit to their sect home but also avoid the city of Jerusalem about five miles north of their destination.

The wise men of Qumran, former mentors of Mary, were very happy to see the progress of her pregnancy. They seemed pleased with the care and attention Joseph rendered the expectant mother. Joseph was, after all, their choice to be keeper of the Holy Mother. The priests urged the couple to leave early the next morning. They feared Mary might give birth before reaching Bethlehem.

The trail west of Qumran traversed rugged desert terrain. For much of the journey, the group followed a dry riverbed. Rocky cliffs lined the way, providing much-welcomed cool and shaded reposes from the desert heat. It was near one of those cliffs that Mary cried for Joseph to stop and find her a place to rest. Joseph noticed an unoccupied cave above the trail. There he left Mary while he went in search of a midwife. Mary was about to give birth.

The cave was about three miles east of Bethlehem.[6]

Suddenly, all became still. Birds stopped in mid-flight. Working people, at a table prepared to eat, froze motionless. Sheep stood apart from each other without moving. Goat kids stood still in the water, but did not drink. The clouds overhead moved in rapid, choppy sequences. It was the instant of birth.

Joseph ran down the hill to hail a woman to help with the birth. He pleaded to the woman that Mary — "educated in the Holy of Holies" — was about to give birth. The woman followed anxiously to the cave. By a stroke of chance, the woman happened to be maid servant of Princess Salomé — the daughter of Herod the Great and dupe ruler of Jamnia, Azotus, Phasaelis and Archelais.

From the cave, a bright light shown. The light increased in intensity until Mary brought the child to her breast. The midwife knew that she had witnessed the birth of a king. She ran from the cave to find Princess Salomé. She excitedly told her mistress that a new King lay in the cave. Salomé followed her slave to the cave to witness the virgin birth.

Salomé was unclean, and unfit to touch the newborn Messiah so, when she reached to touch the baby, her hand was suddenly withered. But Jesus forgave her.

Salomé's hand would not long remain deformed. While still in the cave, she proclaimed her belief that the baby Jesus was the King of Israel; her hand was instantly restored.

Great excitement swept through Bethlehem. The streets were packed with Davidians in the mood for rebellion. Rumors of the birth of the King spread like a desert brush fire. If Herod and the authorities had doubted reports of a planned insurrection, they could not now fail to see. The census edit backfired. Too many discontented people in one small place spelled trouble for the shaky government.

Salomé quickly made her way to the royal quarters in Jerusalem. She breathlessly told King Herod that a child with the claimed credentials to the kingship had been born. Clearly, the census had not accomplished its purpose. Drastic measures were called for.

Herod Archelaus sent deputies to intercept the wise priests who were making their way west from Qumran to confirm the birth of the Messiah and fulfill certain prophesies. Herod ordered the priests to be brought to the royal quarters. There he questioned them about the insurrection. "Who is this child who would claim to be King?" he asked. "Would the people place an unknown child on the throne in my stead, I, son of Herod the Great?"[7]

"God would," the priests answered.

"'And a child shall lead them,' I suppose! But the time is not now — not while I am King." Herod turned to whisper to his general by his side, "I will humor them. You must find the 'King' and kill him."

"I wish to worship him," Herod said aloud to the priests. "How will I know him?"

"A star from heaven shall mark the place where he lies. This was written by the ancient prophets."

Perhaps the wise men expected Herod to joyfully renounce his claim to power and accept the coming King of Israel. More likely, they planned to move the infant Jesus to the safety of the countryside while support for the insurrection grew. Whatever their intentions, they did not anticipate the intensity of Herod's anger and rapidity of his response.

Herod was incensed that his authority might be brought into question. When his soldiers did not quickly find the new king, he angrily instigated a cruel plan. If he could not identify the infant pretender, he would eliminate all possibilities. He ordered every newborn child to be executed. All Davidians, all Ashers, all Galileans, all Judeans and Israelis, all males and all females under the age of two years would be killed.[8]

As Herod's evil edit began to be actualized, Mary, Jesus and Joseph arrived in Bethlehem. When they sought refuge at an Essene home, they learned of the edict. With the help of their host family, they quickly hid Jesus in a manger among camels and goats.

The hiding place in the manger would not long be adequate to protect Mary and Jesus. When the wise men from Qumran were finally led to Jesus, they pleaded with Joseph to take Mary and Jesus and flee Israel and Judea.[9]

There was a fanatical rush to disobey the edict. Newborn babies and pregnant women were hidden in every conceivable place. Most fled Bethlehem and Jerusalem.

In the same week of Jesus' birth, Elizabeth, wife of Zacharias (now High Priest of all Judea and Israel), gave birth in Jerusalem. Elizabeth fled with her new son into the eastern desert. Near Qumran, "... a mountain was divided and received them." They would hide within that mountain until the danger was past. Priests from the monastery brought food, water, and comfort to them for almost *three* years.

Zacharias refused to help Herod's goons round up the infants of Israel. For this, Zacharias was led to the Court of the Priests and killed upon the Holy Altar. His blood flowed upon the rock of the altar, but did not congeal. Seeing this abnormality, his executioners fled in terror.[10]

The mass murder of the newborn Israelites did not go as planned. Many were not found. Of those killed, none proved to be the promised Messiah. An irate Herod ordered even more desperate measures. Hundreds of priests were rounded up and killed. Herod and his death squad were cursed by God. The people would never forget: "On the Sabbath, they committed seven unforgivable sins. They murdered a priest, a prophet and a king. They shed blood of the innocent. They polluted the court."

The land of David teetered on the edge of self-genocide. No leader stepped forward to organize a resistance. An uncle of Jesus, Simeon, was selected 'by lot' to the unwanted position of High Priest of Judea and Israel. He attempted to mediate between Herod and the Davidians but little calm would return until Herod Archelaus died four years later. The Roman garrison at Jerusalem watched the slaughter in amazed horror. What could provoke Jew to kill Jew with such vindictiveness?

The Roman governor at Caesarea acceded to Herod's plea and sent troops to help defeat the insurrection. The dreaded Roman legions now pursued those who defied the rule of Herod. The power of Rome was mobilized to save Herod.

Joseph, Mary and Jesus fled Bethlehem directly eastward down the dry leeward divide toward the Dead Sea, four hundred meters below sea level. Predominant winds blew eastward from the Mediterranean Sea, dropped whatever moisture the air held on its upward sweep over the mountain divide just beyond which Bethlehem had been built and flowed dry and rainless down the barren desert floor to the Dead Sea.

The escape path chosen by Joseph along an old and little-used trader route must have been inspired by God. Other Davidians attempted to hide in the independent city-state of Ascalon by the Great Sea. Their children were soon destroyed as Roman legions ignored the independence of the tiny city.

Romans searched all ship traffic out of Ascalon. They cut apart fleeing columns and slaughtered them as they traveled southward along the main land trade route through Gaza toward Egypt.

Joseph led his charges eastward through the wilderness of Judea. They departed Bethlehem in darkness and arrived at the mountaintop fortress of Masada before nightfall of the second day. There they remained only long enough to obtain camels and take on provision for the long and dangerous journey across the Great Desert to Egypt. Word of Herod's edict had not yet reached the small Roman garrison in that isolated place but Joseph knew Herod's police or the Romans would soon descend upon Masada.

The old overland route made it difficult for heavy chariots and armed infantry to pursue. The little-improved road from Masada traversed southward through Arad, around dangerous Beersheeba, across the river of Egypt near Mt. Jebel Hellal and over the Great Desert to the Sea of Reeds. After the Sea of Reeds — where constant winter mud made chariot travel impossible — was Egypt, their destination.[11]

More dangerous than the Romans were the bands of thieves that infested this old trade route. Halfway across the dry desert, Joseph and Mary were stopped by an armed gang led by Titus and Dumachus. When Titus and Dumachus saw the infant Jesus poking his head from the cloth cradle his mother held, a powerful sense of foredoom overcame them. They saw themselves hanging from crucible crosses backlighted by a fiery red evening sun descending below a barren hillside. Between them was the infant Jesus and Jesus blessed them.

Dumachus moved to kill the baby immediately. If the baby Jesus were dead, how could this evil vision come true?

Titus felt fear and compassion for the baby. "Stop," he cried. "Can you not see this baby is the prophesied Messiah, the hope and promise for the future of Israel? Here take this gold! Go your way. We shall meet again on that lonely hill in Jerusalem."

Another time the escapees were waylaid by a large band of robbers. The presence of Jesus again saved Joseph and Mary. As the thieves neared the helpless pair, intent on robbing and killing them, an odd thing happened. Suddenly the roar of the Roman army was heard and a cloud of dust seen over the horizon. The band of thieves stopped, turned and fled. After they flew in confused fear, the noise and dust disappeared and all was still and peaceful. The thoughts and imaginations of the robbers had been manipulated by an outside force.

Jesus smiled.

Both Joseph and Mary spoke Egyptian. Mary had learned it during the years of study in the monastery and Joseph knew it from work travels as a young man. Knowledge of the language helped them find shelter in the city of Heliopolis. The family moved at ease throughout the land of the pharaohs for the next three years. Many strange and miraculous things occurred in the presence of Jesus and Mary. Mary attributed the many miracles to the baby Jesus. The stories of healing exorcism flourished within Egypt as years passed.

Jesus' physical appearance was itself strange if not awe-inspiring. In accordance with the prophesies of Isaiah, Jesus was never seen with hair; all baby hair was either shaved or absent at birth. Throughout his life, the shiny bald head of Jesus would be a well-known sign of the Messiah to those who read and understood the ancient Scriptures.[12]

Other physical features made Jesus stand out as unique. Jesus never had a baby face. He was born with a fully developed head of an adult. Like the medieval paintings of Diego Velazquez, Jesus appeared as an adult with a strange, miniature body.

Jesus' eyes were a deep sea of blue. To look into the eyes of Jesus was to peer into an endless cavern of knowledge. Hypnotic control of all who approached him seemed to be a magical ability of the infant Jesus, an ability that he would certainly retain into adulthood.

The home in which Joseph, Mary and Jesus lodged the first few days after arriving in Heliopolis was that of one of the very few Essene families in Egypt. The Essene faith made them very much want to experience the coming of the Messiah, but they doubted that this strange-looking baby could be that savior. Mary insisted that they approach Jesus and speak to him. They asked, "How can we speak with a babe in the cradle?"

The baby Jesus answered them in a clear, full-throated adult voice. "Speak to me of life. I am the Savior. I was blessed by God, itself. I shall be blessed on the day of my death when I shall rise to be with my father. Know me. I am He."[13]

Jesus never spoke as a baby again. His growth seemed to be normal but many sinister occurrences marked his infancy.

The Egyptian Essene family asked Joseph and Mary to leave their home and to take Jesus with them. They clearly feared that the baby Jesus was a sorcerer who would bring evil unto their home.

As Joseph and Mary walked the streets of Heliopolis carrying Jesus, public monuments to false gods fell and crumbled behind them. Ensigns held by guards at government buildings dipped in salute against all efforts of the soldiers to hold them upright. In contrast, an aura of power shined from the baby Jesus.

A demented woman broke her binding chains and ran naked in the streets. She threw rocks and shouted at every man she met. When Mary saw and blessed this woman in the name of Jesus, the demon fled her body. The woman's grateful family then fed, lodged and resupplied the travelers.

The family moved up the Nile toward Thebes. Along the way, Mary studied magic from Egyptian magi and learned what she could of Gnostic mysticism. Mary herself and Jesus were gaining reputations as accomplished magicians.[14]

In one town, a young bride had been struck dumb and unable to solemnize her recent marriage. When the girl's mother allowed her to hold and kiss Jesus, the bride suddenly spoke and praised God. The grateful wedding party fed, housed and entertained the travelers for three days.

The next settlement was near the King's summer quarters. Its best-know resident was a woman possessed by Satan. Every night, Satan entered the woman as a snake. Mary told the woman that she could help. "Touch the child," she commanded, "You shall be healed." The woman held Jesus in her arms. At that moment, She knew that Satan would never again possess her.

A maid-servant of the Queen next approached Mary and Jesus. This young girl was inflicted with the dreaded leprosy. Mary did not appear to fear the disease. She asked the girl to disrobe. Mary then took the water in which Jesus had bathed. She anointed the girl with the water. The sores left the body as would caked dirt. The girl was grateful beyond measure.

The maid-servant proved to be instrumental in elevating Jesus' family to a privileged position in the land of the Nile. When she returned to the Queen's services, clear of all signs of leprosy, the royal family was amazed. They asked by what method she had been cured. The one hope to continue their royal lineage might be Jesus and Mary.

The King and Queen had kept a dark, painful secret from their subjects. They had a leprous son whom they could not present to the people because the Word said that such an infirmity as leprosy proved a person to be sinful and thus cursed by God. The King and Queen knew their sin was having had sexual intercourse before marriage. They commanded the maid-servant to bring Mary and Jesus to their quarters.

"Do you believe this baby is King of the Jews?" Mary asked.

"We do," they answered. "We must," they thought.

"When he is crowned, will you accept him as ruler of all Israel and Judea? Do you promise not to invade our land?"

"We will always be friends, if only our son can be made whole. We will insure your stay in the land of Egypt is comfortable and pleasant. We believe! Jesus is the Messiah of the Jewish people."

Mary smiled. "Go, Go to the bed chambers of your young son. He shall be King of Egypt. Your act of confession, your belief that Jesus is the Messiah of the Jews, has made your son whole. The monarchy is preserved."

The respect and friendship gained as a result of this miraculous act meant that Joseph and Mary would no longer worry about food and lodging while in Egypt. They enjoyed the comfort and hospitality of the finest households along the Great River. Many of those rich families suffered trial and hardships hidden from the general populace.

In one royal house, a young man who was in line to inherit a very large estate had been transformed into a mule by a jealous woman witch. Mary entered the private quarters of the large house and saw the mule-boy's sisters crying. After she heard and understood the sad story of love gone wrong, she placed the baby Jesus upon the back of the mule. Immediately, the mule returned to the shape of a handsome young lover.

The mule-boy story could not be told to the common people because royal families never allowed their internal problems to be known. Nevertheless, Mary and Joseph became good friends with this rich family. This added to their ease of movement within Egyptian society.

Mary, Joseph and Jesus lodged at the house of a newly married couple who seemed very disdainful. The bride confided to Mary that her husband was unable to perform the act of sex. Mary gave the bride some unusual advice. "Tonight, sleep against that wall. I will place Jesus against the wall opposite your bed. Lie with your husband. Your marriage will be consummated. You shall conceive."

That night, while Jesus slept, the husband became whole and planted the seed of fatherhood.

Along the Nile, Mary and Jesus became known as magical physicians. Demons were cast out, the lame walked, withered limbs became whole, and spent bodies were nourished. The family was welcomed into the best of homes wherever they traveled. A good life seemed assured, but the honing of the art of creating perception over reality was intended to further a more noble objective than just obtaining food, shelter and comfort.

A messenger arrived from the land of David. "King Herod Archelaus is dead. His war of genocide is over. Return home to the promised land of God. We will rebuild and milk and honey shall flow in the streets of Jerusalem."

Joseph confessed to Mary, "I miss my children. We must go back home. It is surely safe now."

"Yes," replied Mary. "Jesus is three years old. It is time to be educated in the law. This strange land is no place for the Messiah. We must return him to his people."

"The Pharaoh has promised us the best camels and an escort across the Great Desert. We will return along the main trade route. A journey by sea can be dangerous this time of year."

"So say you."

"We must prepare well. God will go with us," Joseph said, then turned to instruct his slaves. "Make ready the van," he commanded.

Elizabeth called her son John.[15] They remained within the mountain, attended by priests from Qumran, until the death of

Herod Archelaus. Elizabeth then placed the now fatherless John in the monastery to be educated in the way of the Book.

John learned well, but his conversations with God showed him that the ritual cleansing of the Essenes was not adequate to wash away the sins of mortal man. A one-time confession before man and prayer to God for forgiveness followed by a complete immersion under water was essential to receive the Holy Ghost. John's one time baptism in clean river water differed from that of his Essene teachers who practiced frequent ceremonial baptism in holy water within the confines of the temple.

Perhaps physical environment had something to do with John's convictions concerning baptism. While yet a young child, John would often slip outside the walls of the monastery and explore the adjoining desert. As he grew older, his treks became longer and longer. By age twelve, John made trips lasting weeks at a time. His favorite terrain was along the River Jordan just a few miles north of its slow release into the Dead Sea.

At age fourteen, John left the monastery. While he was well-learned in the Torah, Talmud and Essene Word, he resembled a traditional priest in no way. He shunned priestly robes in favor of wild animal skins. His dietary habits included wild berries, locusts, roaches, snakes and clay, hardly the diet of the piously correct. He never wore shoes. His hair was unkempt. He would shout in unknown tongues whenever the spirit so moved. He did not enter a profession and wait until age thirty before teaching the Word as was required by Essene tradition. Instead, he began preaching at age fourteen to all who would come to him. He was the one crying in the wilderness. John lived alone among the rocks and caves of the north Judean wilderness from age fourteen until his execution at age thirty-two. There he taught the law of God as he understood it and practiced one-time baptism. His fame grew as more and more people sought him out to supplement the stale teaching of the official priestly authorities.

John was known as John the Baptist. Some called him the Messiah, but he never claimed to be King of Israel nor did he lead an insurgency to overthrow the Romans and the Herod family. He was betrayed by Salomé, jealous of his following, and murdered by her brother. His head was displayed in the city center.

John did live long enough to meet the man who claimed to be the Messiah. Before he began his campaign, Jesus would seek out his second cousin to receive the Holy Ghost through baptism.

Youth

.

"Then the parents of the dead boy going to Joseph complained, saying, 'You are not fit to live with us, in our city, having such a boy as that.'"
        Lost Books of the Bible, "Infancy II" 2:11.

The return journey to the Land of David lacked the elements of danger and hardship of the flight three years before. The van included slaves carrying provisions fit for the highest royalty. King's soldiers flanked the precious cargo, Jesus, for most of the distance. Wayside inns welcomed the travelers at points equal to an easy days camel ride. Cool breezes blew onshore from the Mediterranean Sea, never more than a few miles north of their eastward route. Many trade caravans met them along this well-traveled road.

At the small port city of Rhinocolura, Egyptian guards bade farewell, and turned back toward their homeland. It was only a short three day ride from Rhinocolura, through Raphia, Gaza and Marisa to Bethlehem.

Bethlehem was not the happy, joyful place they anticipated. A cold, misty silence hung over the city as they approached it toward the south gate.The cough of death, carried by Roman soldiers from the cold, damp region called Gaul, swept through Israel and Judea. The people of David did not have immune systems conditioned to fight the deadly influenza. Children, especially, succumbed to its insidious incursion.

A flow of refugees met our travelers as they neared the city. The inbound caravan stood out as conspicuously wealthy. The fine camels, the servant attendants, the finery — all indicated that Joseph and his charge were not poor. The southbound wretched pleaded to Joseph and Mary. "Miserere! Do not enter the city," they warned. "Death lurks there."

The van continued toward Bethlehem. There was no fear in Mary or Joseph. "We must help. Our birthright from King David demands we help. The people of David must survive," said Mary.

"God will protect us," Joseph assured her.

"God will save the City of David," Mary added.

A dark frail woman dressed entirely in black wept over her child beside the road, "He is dead," she wailed. "Why did God do this?"

"God does not wish to harm you," Mary counseled her from high atop her mount. "This affliction has been brought onto Israel for sins of omission. Israel must work harder to bring on the Kingdom."

"What can I, a poor helpless woman, do?"

"You must first believe."

"I do. I do believe."

"Here,"Mary threw down Jesus' swaddling clothes, take this. Wrap your baby in it. No harm will come to you or your baby. Go with God."

"Daughter of God," the poor woman muttered in thanks.

As the van moved away from the woman toward the city, Mary heard joyful shouts from the woman. "He is well. My baby lives! God go with you."[1]

At the water well that marked the city center, Joseph drew the little caravan to a halt. The camels and servants rushed to the water trough to drink that fluid of life. Joseph and Mary disrobed to cleanse themselves before seeking an Essene home for lodging.

Mary was bathing Jesus in a small wooden tub when a desperate woman approached her. "Your servants tell me you are Holy Mary, the physician. Your fame has spread throughout the land. Can you not cure the sick and affected? You must help me. My son is sick and will surely die. Please, heal my son."

"Your faith will heal your son. If you believe it so, so it is," Mary explained. "Take a little of this water with which I have bathed my son Jesus. Sprinkle it on your son. It will wash away the demon that possesses him."

The woman did as Mary instructed. The fever immediately left her baby and he began to laugh and play. The miracle of faith once again defeated the evil demons that cause illness and death.

A neighbor of the woman whose sucking son was healed also had a young child afflicted with the strange new diseases. When she was told of Mary and Jesus, she immediately sought them out. She found Mary and Jesus in an Essene home that served as an inn for the advocates of the sect who traveled to Bethlehem.

Mary had retained some of the water in which she washed Jesus. The woman held out her son for Mary to see. His eyes were swollen shut; his brain racked with pain. He was too near death to cry. Mary took a cloth, wet with Jesus' bath water, and wiped the infant boy's hot brow. The boy smiled, opened his eyes and began to cry a healthy cry.

The mother was overcome with joy. She fell to her knees and kissed Mary's robe. "It is a miracle," the woman cried.

"You are God Incarnate. I worship you with all my being. What can I do to please you, to repay you for my son?"

"I am not God," Mary said. "You have only to praise the single God and give thanks to Him. It is your faith in the power of God that cured your son."

Mary then made a strange request of the woman. "Tell no one of this occurrence. If they ask how your son was cured, only say, 'I believe in the power of the single God.' Never admit you have met Jesus and me."

Perhaps Mary feared an onslaught of patients seeking relief or perhaps she thought the time not ready to reveal Jesus as Messiah. Whatever the reason, she could not long hide the ability of infant Jesus to effect cures.

In the Essene household that welcomed the travelers Joseph, Mary and Jesus, two women shared wifely duties. They were married to the same man, the husband of one having taken his deceased older brother's wife, as was the custom. However, neither woman was pleased with this arrangement.

One of the two wives was called Mary and her infant son's name was Caleb. Unknown to the Holy Mother Mary, this Mary obtained a piece of Jesus' swaddling cloth by trading a carpet for it with one of Joseph's servants. A carpet was a precious possession for even rich families. With the old swaddling cloth, she made a coat for her baby Caleb. When she dressed her baby in the coat, his severe distemper was cured, but the equally sick son of the other wife died. The grieved mother plotted to even the score.

When Mary, mother of Caleb, left the house to get oatmeal for baking bread, her rival wife threw the child Caleb into the hot oven and ran into the rear garden. Upon her return to the kitchen, Mary found the oven cold and her baby laughing and playing in it, unhurt. Jesus stood nearby.

Again, the grieving mother tried to kill Caleb. She caught him beside the city water well and threw him into it. After she left the scene, two men came to the well to draw water. They were amazed to see the baby sitting on top of the water in the well, alive and happy.

Caleb's mother suspected her rival wife was attempting to kill her son. She asked Holy Mary for aid and advice. Mary told her not to fear. "God will vindicate your injured cause," she said.

After talking to Jesus' mother, Mary, mother of Caleb, left her home to fetch some water. At the city center, she noticed a crowd of excited people gathered around the water well.

The people were looking at a dead woman in the well. When the rival wife had come to draw water, her foot became entangled in the rope and the heavy bucket pulled her headlong into the gruesome death hole, crushing her skull and many bones. The dead wife could never again defy the will of God. Caleb's mother received revenge at the precise moment that Holy Mary had promised vindication.

Mary's reputation as a physician/magician grew. Many mothers sought her out to heal their desperately ill children. She received each of the children by sprinkling water on them, water in which Jesus had been bathed. All were cured. Mary asked every mother to give thanks to God and to remember Jesus.

One mother in the ravaged city brought two sons to Mary. One was dead and the other was very sick. Mary felt compassion for the pitiful woman, instructing her to place the dead child beside the sleeping Jesus. The instant the child's body touched Jesus, the child awoke and became well. Thus, Nathaniel Bartholomew, a son of a royal family, lived to testify to the power of the single God and become a zealot in the Davidian cause.

The mother's other child was also cured. They were cured because their mother believed them to be cured. Reality was as it was perceived. Reality proved to be in the mind of the beholder.

A three year old child, whom many accepted as King, was establishing a base of support for the insurrection that was sure to follow. As long as Herod retained Roman sanctions to power the would-be oligarchy based on Davidian descent was powerless. The Herodians were considered crude and classless by the old royal establishment. It was only natural that the old royalty would court a potential king. Conversely, the support of the old royalty was essential for the success of any insurgency. The old royal establishment was utilized for financial and material support during the insurgency and would be needed for bureaucratic and entrepreneurial expertise after a successful overthrow of the contemporary ruling establishment.

One bride of a prince who was betrothed but not yet married through sexual intercourse came to Holy Mary for help. "I am cursed," she told Mary. "The Prince will not lie with me. When we entered the bed chamber to consummate our marriage, he saw the marks of leprosy upon my body. Why am I so cursed?"

"Daughter of God," Mary consoled, "it is for a purpose that you are here. You must believe that Jesus is the King."

"That I have been told by others. I am here because others say Jesus heals."

"But do you believe?"

"I do."

"Will you accept him as King of Israel?"

"I will and I do."

"Stand here and drop your robe," Mary commanded.

The sores stood out on a young body never exposed to the sun, her shoulders, down the tops of her small girlish breasts, inside her arms and thighs. There stood a young soul doomed to years of isolation and a slow, tortuous death. The girl remained motionless, hands limply dangling at her side, head bowed. Her shame was that the demon that inflicted her would leave such positive proof.

Mary approached the girl to pour a pan of water over the head and shoulders of the soft young body. Mary gently distributed the water with her hand, insuring that every inch was wetted by the healing fluid. The sores quickly disappeared.

"Go with God," she commanded. "Praise to the single God. Remember Jesus."

The young woman would not forget Jesus, nor would the prince who now accepted her as his wife. This princely family could be called upon for active support when the time came to overthrow the Herodian government.

An astonishing incident provided a climax to the story of the prince and his bride. The new wife at her toilet handed the damp robe to her leprous attendant. The attendant draped the robe over her shoulder and was cured—cured without a confession of personal faith. The faith of her mistress was enough to heal the Gentile slave.

Certainty of the power of Jesus and Mary began to spread outward from the city of David. The prince's new bride visited a cousin who lived not far from Bethlehem. The cousin's young daughter suffered from dementia, Satan living within her as a dragon. Her emaciated body was undernourished to the point of death. Her mother and father mourned for her. They asked all they met who could help rid their daughter of this curse. The prince's wife told them of Jesus and Mary.

The mother and father of the possessed girl brought her to Jesus and Mary in Bethlehem. Mary asked what troubled them. They presented their daughter. Mary knew what to do. She gave them a swaddling cloth that she had soaked in the bathwater of young Jesus.

The hopeful family returned home to await an attack by Satan on their daughter. When the girl began a seizure, they gave the swaddling cloth to her. She wrapped it around her head causing the Devil to pour out of her mouth with fire and burning coals. A simple swaddling cloth of Jesus overcame the Devil himself.

Three months passed in that city of David. The epidemic ran its course of serious childhood distemper. It was time to move on to the Nazareth region of Galilee—home. Jesus had just begun to reach the age of recollection. He would meet his half-brothers and sisters for the first time.

James, Joseph, Simon, Judas Thaddeus and two sisters met the voyagers at the gate of their spacious yet plain home.[2] Leah, the faithful maidservant and her husband, Muhammad Abdul, trailed smiling behind the children of Joseph. All animal indicators of wealth—the camels, goats, sheep, even chickens recently introduced to the area—appeared healthy and fertile.

Mary often visited the Roman legion garrison near their home. She was a beautiful mature woman of nineteen years. Joseph was forty-three, weather-beaten, stooped and preoccupied with his commercial endeavors. Mary soon became pregnant with her second child. When the child was born, it remarkably resembled Jesus. He and Jesus were the only blue-eyed children in the region. Mary named her new baby boy Thomas the Twin.

Jesus knew that there was something special about himself. His mother constantly told him so. Mary was convinced that her child was the promised Messiah. All her education in the Essene monastery had prepared her to raise and educate her child to be the new king. The old ruling order faced the end of their days and they knew it. The new order promised a bright new kingdom that would endure forever. The success or failure of the promise rested squarely upon the will of Mary. Unlike most Israelite boys who attended public schools, the education of the Messiah was mainly a product of his mother. The Essene priests of Qumran were more than happy with the results.

Mary taught Jesus much more than the traditional learning of the rich and refined. He did learn Greek. He learned to speak and write the dialect of Jerusalem, shunning the coarse, guttural Aramaic that marked the common people of the Galilean countryside. Much of his young life was devoted to study of the ancient teachers of monotheism. He knew, almost by heart, the laws, myths and commandments of what we now know as the Old Testament. Jesus absorbed the values of the Essene sect that required a plain and unpretentious life, generosity to all, observance of the law and faith that God could provide for all daily needs. But he learned much more — much that would shape his character and teaching.

Jesus learned the mystical secrets of a magus physician. He became a master of the healing powers of suggestion. He learned well that to believe one's self whole or happy or free of demons often made it so. The power to heal and drive out demons was not only essential to convince the populace he was the promised Messiah, but it must have also erased any doubts Jesus might have entertained that he just might be a normal man. Jesus was not the first, the only or the last person to demonstrate the power to heal by sheer force of personality. However, he used his power more purposefully than most.

The almost constant tutelage of Mary allowed Jesus little time to develop interpersonal skills. His childhood was almost entirely stolen from him. He became very withdrawn and self-focused. His powerful intellect whirled inward like a huge black hole in the cosmos while his thoughts and studies pulled inside himself to congeal into a coherent philosophy that could change the world. His philosophy outlined a way of living intended to be an integral part of the new Kingdom when he reached manhood.

Given his forced isolation during youth, it is little wonder that Jesus became somewhat introverted. Constant study and limited time spent with his father helped shape his personal values. He was a mother-centered boy. What little time he did enjoy in his interpersonal child's play was often troubled. He knew he was special. His mother told him that. She told him the stories of his magical healing as a baby in Egypt and how he had spoken from the cradle to proclaim his holy status. She told him he was fathered by the Holy Ghost to be King. His blue eyes and bald head set him apart physically from other young boys. As he learned to read the many spiritual prognostications, vaguely written and shrouded in mysterious syntax that could be understood by a reader according to his own needs, imagination — and Mary — told him those scriptures predicted his future. When the boy king went outside to play, not yet fully matured as a righteous teacher, problems ensued. The boy Jesus was often accused of black magic. He seemed to be subject to the same impetuosity of youth as any other child, sometimes succumbing to the hateful vindication of the not-yet wise. He used magic in an attempt to build self-esteem and raise his status in the eyes of his peers. Youth was a learning process for Jesus.

When he was seven, Jesus was sometimes allowed to play alongside a nearby creek. The creek, with its gently flowing water and fine clay banks, was a favorite playground for area boys. The clay was great for molding shapes. Jesus would sit aside from the other boys, alone, creating clay images that he imagined were part of his future kingdom. Jesus was clearly more creative than the other boys. His depictions of asses, oxen, birds and sparrows were perfect in every detail. The boys grouped together and conspired to humiliate Jesus. They broke huddle and turned toward him, gaining courage from each other. "Sissy boy. Why is your skin so white?"

"Look, he has no hair! His eyes are filled with blue water."

"He plays with silly toys.I will kick them over."

The bravest boy moved menacingly toward the clay objects. Jesus stopped him with his eyes. The young king stared into the frightened eyes of the belligerent. Jesus raised his open right hand over the clay imagery. "Live. Live. I command you. Live." The objects moved.The asses brayed, the oxen walked and the birds flew away, or at least this appeared to happen in the hypnotized eyes of the boys.

The gang turned and ran directly to their parents. "He is a sorcerer," they yelled. "The white-skinned boy, he is evil."

After hearing the story, the boys' parents forbade them to play with or to approach Jesus who became more withdrawn and committed to understanding the learning his mother thrust upon him.

A few months later as Jesus walked down a dry dusty street, he saw the little gang of boys run and hide. They ran into a neighbor woman's house and hid in a large furnace used to process sugar cane into sugar. Jesus made an unwise decision to use his power to dislodge them. He shouted to them by name. They answered with the voices of three-year olds. Not satisfied, he shouted at them again. "You kids. Come out so we may see what beautiful coats you have."

The door of the furnace opened and what had entered as young boys scurried out as little goat kids. The women of the house were amazed at what they thought they saw. Momentarily, Jesus gestured to the goats and their perceived shape changed back into that of normal boys. All in the room, the boys and the women, worshipped Jesus in fear.

The boys now played with Jesus, but certainly not on a basis of equality. Jesus was King and the boys were his subjects. Jesus thought, "The children of Israel are simple fools like the Ethiopians of Upper Egypt."

Jesus became the kingly leader of an expanding gang of boys. They crowned him with flowers. He in turn assigned rank and position to each of them. This organization, formed by Jesus when he was less than ten years old, served as the foundation for an active insurgency twenty-two years later.

When other boys passed near the gang's self-proclaimed territory, Jesus' wards would kidnap them and force them to worship him as King. They were often rough and disrespectful of other boys, but there were many times Jesus used his power for good.

Two of the gang member's lives were saved by Jesus. They remained with Jesus as trusted lieutenants until his death. The first was Judas Iscariot.

Judas Iscariot was a six year old boy possessed by Satan when his mother brought him to the eight year old Jesus. He walked around as if crazy and bit everyone he could catch. If no one was near him, he bit himself. His arms and feet were bloody from self-inflicted wounds. He was filthy beyond description — wild hair, body caked with mud, saliva and blood, near naked, no shoes. His mother feared to touch him. Jesus walked over, sat down beside him and reached out to touch him. Judas tried to bite the hand of Jesus. Jesus grabbed the rough hair of Judas to prevent sharp teeth from reaching his skin. Judas struck Jesus hard in the right side, making Jesus scream. Satan responded to the scream of Jesus by flying out from Judas' body.

Satan never returned to Judas, whose grateful mother, still fearful, left Judas to be raised by Mary and Joseph. Judas and Jesus were close childhood buddies. Because they were seen together so often in a loving relationship and Judas lived in the household as a full family member, many people thought they were blood brothers. They were not but their comradeship became just as close and binding as that of brothers.[3]

Not far from the secret cave where Jesus held court over his youthful gang, a young boy named Simon played and gathered wood for a family fire. Simon reached into a bird nest only to be bitten by a poisonous snake hiding there. He yelled for help and slumped into a still position. His companions ran to get adult help. Some neighbors went to Simon and carried him toward the city. As the group passed along the road near Jesus and his youthful followers, Jesus spotted the comatose boy. He commanded the neighbors to position the limp body near his rock throne while his subjects rushed to capture the snake. The boys returned with the snake, presenting it to Jesus who held it high. His first finger and thumb gripped it tightly behind the neck for the assembling crowd to see. He commanded the snake to suck the venom from the body of Simon. Much to the horror of the neighbors who hoped to save Simon, he thrust open its mouth onto the spot swollen from its poison. Simon immediately revived as the snake did what Jesus ordered. Jesus then killed the snake with a verbal curse. The boy, Simon the Canaanite, swore allegiance to Jesus and became a lifelong member of the gang.

Jesus also saved his half-brother James from a venomous snake bite. The two were playing alone when a snake hit James' leg. He remained very quiet and still while Jesus blew upon the bite. Although the fang marks could still be seen, the leg never swelled and James never became sick. James, always a loving older brother, later became a disciple of Jesus.

Another time the boys were playing on a housetop. One boy was thrown from the roof and died. The remaining boys ran away leaving Jesus alone to face the relatives who came running. The relatives naturally accused Jesus of killing their kin. Jesus said to them that the dead boy should tell them who killed him. "Tell them. For the sake of future Israel, tell them who pushed you."

Zeinus, the dead boy, clearly communicated the name of the culprit who had pushed him and fell back into everlasting rest. All who thought they saw and heard this praised God for a miracle.

Once, the young Jesus allowed his earthly vengeful ego to overpower a not yet mature messianic personality. Jesus made some sparrows of clay beside a pool the boys had made. It was Sunday. Jesus clapped his hand over the clay birds and watched them come alive and fly away. The pious son of Hanani, a self-righteous Pharisee, saw the little exercise of magical powers. Less than impressed, the son of Hanani condemned this "labor" Jesus performed on the Sabbath. He kicked the makeshift dam and released the pool of water. Angered, Jesus said to him, "As the water has vanished from this pool, so shall you vanish from this earth." The boy fell dead.

Jesus employed his power in a good way to help his father Joseph who was not a very good carpenter. His eyes were now weak and his hands shaky. He often mis-measured small construction projects. Jesus would wave his hand over whatever project Joseph had mis-cut and it would change into the intended shape.

Although his carpentry skill was barely adequate, Joseph's economic status positioned him to receive contracts to work for other royalty and present members of the ruling party. King Herod Antipas, ruler of Galilee and Peraca, commissioned a very important project. Joseph was to carve a delicate, ornate throne out of imported teakwood for the pretender king. The design was so complicated it took Joseph two years to complete. Herod's police arrived to pick up the new throne after Joseph sent word it was finished. They found it three inches too narrow for their rather large master. Jesus comforted Joseph and told him that together they could fix it. Jesus put his hands on one side of the throne and directed Joseph to put his on the other side. They pulled until the wood appeared to stretch to its proper size. The police were amazed. They no doubt returned to Herod with the story of Jesus' power as well as the throne.

A man known as Salem was the best dyer in all of Galilee. He learned his trade in the secretive shops of Tyre. His colors were sharp, brilliant and varied. Even Jesus marvelled at the work of the master craftsman. Salem was related to Jesus through his mother's lineage.

One day Jesus passed Salem's dye shop. As Salem was nowhere to be seen, Jesus decided to engage in a bit of mischief. He threw all of the cloth that was ready to be dyed into a hot stove. Salem soon returned and roared unmercifully at Jesus. Jesus told him not to worry and took all the cloth out of the hot oven. Salem was amazed to see each cloth not only unburned but also dyed to the exact color each customer had ordered. At least, all of this appeared so in the eyes of Salem. Later, Jesus apprenticed under Salem and became a dyer himself.

In the course of Jesus' formative education, Mary twice attempted to employ the services of Greek educators. She felt that classic Greek teaching would benefit the future king.

The first Greek teacher was Zaccheus of the Nazareth area. Zaccheus began the instruction of seven year old Jesus with the Greek alphabet. Jesus proceeded to not only recite the entire alphabet but also to explain the historical meaning of each letter. Zaccheus told Mary that Jesus had no need for more learning and went on his way.

Another Greek schoolmaster was much more energetic in his approach to instructing Jesus, commanding that Jesus repeat the alphabet aloud.

"Aleph," Jesus answered, then asked "Teacher, what is the meaning of the letter, Aleph?" Jesus well knew the answer to this question. He only wanted to test the patience of this potential tutor.

"I will not answer," griped the schoolmaster. "I am the teacher and you are the student. Now you tell me the meaning of the first letter."

"I asked you first. You must answer me. I am the master."

"You are not the master yet. I am the master here." The schoolmaster lifted his arm to strike Jesus. "You shall never again attempt to hit a child with that hand," Jesus stated.

The schoolmaster dropped the stick he held. He looked at his hand in horror. Still held high in readiness to strike, it was withered beyond use. He screamed in fear. His eyes glowed with hate for the little sorcerer. He lunged at Jesus but never touched him. The schoolmaster slumped dead at the feet of the eight year old king.

Mary and Joseph decided that Jesus could best be educated by them at home. Between eight and twelve years of age, Jesus spent most of his time at home studying under the tutelage of Mary. Because he was so little seen, some believed that he traveled back to Egypt to study but that was not necessary. His mother taught him all a righteous leader would need to know: languages, law, astronomy, physics, philosophy, magic and metaphysics. At age twelve, he was tested by learned priests in Jerusalem prior to economic apprenticeship. Law and tradition required that a rabbi follow a pre-ordained course of instruction until age twelve. After that came testing, an apprenticeship, several years of productive labor in a learned skill while fathering children for Israel and studying the law. Finally, at age thirty, the candidate could assume the role of wise and learned teacher.

For three days the priests, each an expert in one field of study, questioned Jesus. He answered each question and often posed a query of his own. His understanding of the law and spiritual matters amazed the priests. They were pleased. Jesus did not have to tell them, "It is time I be about my father's business." They knew. The Kingdom of David was at hand.[4]

Dye Shop Conspiracy

"Jesus said, 'Perhaps people think I have come to impose peace upon the world. They do not know that I have come to impose conflicts upon the earth: fire, sword, war. For there will be five in a house: There will be three against two and two against three, father against son and son against father, and they will stand alone.'"

The Gospel of Thomas, 16.

Young Jesus returned to the Nazarene area to begin his apprenticeship in the art of dyeing under Salem. He continued to study the Scriptures while learning the secrets of Tyrean color. He never fulfilled the commandment to grow and be fruitful. He never produced a son for Israel. Only as an Essene could Jesus successfully pursue the call to teach and still maintain manhood celibacy. The Essene sect tolerated, even encouraged, celibacy in its priesthood while other religious traditions required marriage.[1]

Jesus often left the little village of Nazareth to spend long hours in the nearby city of Sepphoris. In that prominently Greek city, he could test his intellect against learned scholars of philosophy. He listened and learned. There he perfected the parable method of teaching and gained respect for a more humanistic approach to life than would have been allowed under strict Jewish law. As would any inquisitive youth, Jesus absorbed, assimilated, combined and culled ideals and beliefs in an attempt to satisfy his personal understanding of life. Around a nucleus of harsh Judaism, Jesus added elements of Greek political democracy, Egyptian Gnosticism,[2] oriental tolerance, Galilean pauperism and Essene beliefs of apocalypse. His powerful intellect and relentless quest for truth did not please the Temple establishment. Jesus was never ordained Rabbi.

After a seven year apprenticeship, Jesus was commissioned an artisan dyer but he seemed little interested in that art. He opened a dye shop in the new city of Tiberias[3] that became more *lyceum* or public meeting place than commercial enterprise. The shop often filled with Jesus' childhood buddies and some commercial fishermen who were blessed with Greek educations.

Tiberias, a beautiful city on the western shore of the Sea of Galilee, was built by Caesar Tiberias as a family retreat. Its access to a good highway leading westward made it an ideal market for fisherman from other communities around the small Sea of Galilee—notably Capernaum.

The small group that met in Jesus' dye shop became known by the local population as Nazarenes. They were, however, hardly village peasants. Most were educated, economically secure yet angry. As they feverishly discussed politics, religion and philosophy, the 'evil priests' of the Herod government became more and more the focus of their anger. Those evil priests of the Temple corrupted the people with desecrated teachings, cowed to the Roman occupiers, stole from the poor and lived fat, gluttonous lives. Their blasphemy would not go unpunished in the new world envisioned by Jesus and his close friends. Insurgency was right. Rebellion was a moral duty.

Around the table in the back room of the dye shop were young men who could change the course of history, including Nathaniel Bartholomew,[4] son of the out-of-power noble Talmai family of Galilee. His father imported precious oils and spices from the east via an Armenian trade route. Bartholomew, well-educated in the Greek tradition, was committed to Jesus since the youthful incident in which Jesus saved him from death. A member of the adolescent gang that Jesus had led, Bartholomew's brotherly love of Jesus and devotion to the cause were invaluable. His family wealth and prestige could always be tapped.

Judas Iscariot was also a childhood companion of Jesus and a sometimes member of the original gang.[5] Although Judas considered himself a Judean, he spent long periods in Galilee and was often present at the discussions. Judas knew many wealthy traders and merchants in and around Jerusalem and Jericho. He studied to become a money lender and tax collector as had his father before him. His business contacts were a necessary aid to the earthly financing of the large covert operation that was soon to materialize. As the time approached to commence active campaigning, Judas spent much time in the camp of John the Baptist on the River Jordan. Judas was totally devoted to the cause of a free, God-directed Kingdom of David. His love for Jesus would never falter.

James the Younger was the last child of Joseph and his first wife Mary, before she was abducted to be the mother of Zebedee's children.[6] As half-brother to Jesus, he grew of age with the same visions of a New Kingdom as did Jesus. In the back room, he would argue insurgent tactics with the same fever pitch as he did theology. After the death of Jesus, he would become an early teacher and writer in Jerusalem.

Judas Thaddeus was another half-brother of Jesus by the marriage of Joseph and his first wife, Mary.[7] He was an intense revolutionary. Like James the Younger, he was raised with Jesus in the family home of Joseph and Holy Mary. Bitter memories of the pain and humiliation his mother suffered on behalf of Salomé fired his deep hatred of the ruling Herod family. His was no voice of moderation in the conversations.

Simon Peter the Rock worked as a fisherman but his avocation seemed always to be an insurgent leader.[8] By the time Jesus and his youth gang reached their twenties, Peter was established in the town of Capernaum about ten miles by water from Tiberias. He was considered uneducated although he understood several languages in addition to his native Amorite. He traveled a great deal, owned at least one large fishing boat with hired crews and studied Roman military tactics and the disposition of Roman troops in Israel, Judea and Galilee. He usually sold his catch in Tiberias. Through Andrew, he met Jesus and began to participate in the group discussions.

Andrew was the brother of Simon Peter.[9] Andrew, more pious and less practical than his brother, was also a fisherman in the tradition of their father, Jonas. Andrew left home to follow John the Baptist. It was John the Baptist who told Andrew of the Nazarene organization. The rich and prosperous sons of Jonas, Andrew and Simon Peter were welcome assets to the infant insurgency.

After she was taken from Joseph by Salomé, Herod and Zebedee, Mary gave birth to two males. One was called James Boanorges and the other John Boanorges.[10] Salomé little appreciated the children, leaving the boys often unattended at the couple's royal retreat in Tiberias. The boys often slipped away from their tutor to fish in the bountiful Sea of Galilee.

When Mary was deemed too old to produce more sons for the Herod clan, she found herself under the care of Cleophas, the son of a well-known businessman. He was younger than either Joseph or Zebedee. Because James Boanorges and his brother John were so often seen in the home of Mary and Cleophas in Nazareth, Cleophas was often thought of as their father. Cleophas knew Jesus from birth and became one of his followers.

Given their confusing upbringing, it is little wonder that James Boanorges and John Boanorges turned against the ruling Herod family to become revolutionaries. Even though they were only a few years older than Jesus, they were not his companions during youth. As they reached maturity, they became commercial fishermen out of Capernaum. As fishermen, they became good friends of Andrew and Simon Peter. By persuasion of Andrew and Simon Peter, they began to meet with the Nazarene group whose views suited their temperaments and they became valuable assets. Their zeal, wealth and community position assured them a welcome place in what was becoming the dye shop conspiracy.

Philip[11] was a childhood friend of Andrew and Simon Peter. They all grew up in the provincial city of Bethsaida before Capernaum sprouted a short distance down the northern coast of the Sea of Galilee. Philip, when a pre-puberty youth, had once met Jesus and Nathaniel Bartholomew. He liked to tell the story of Jesus saving Bartholomew's life under a fig tree. Philip was an excellent horseman and a member of the revolutionary Zealots. He was introduced to the dye shop group only a few weeks before all of them pledged their lives and resources to the central objective of overthrowing the government. He quickly saw that this group promised to advance the revolutionary objectives of the Zealots and happily added his pledge.

With Philip, another half-brother of Jesus joined the group. This son of Joseph and his first wife Mary had been actively engaged in underground insurgent warfare for years. Jesus had last seen him as a boy in Nazareth. The family knew him as Simon the Zealot.[12] Simon came to the group a dedicated rebel, ready and willing to give his life to overthrow the Roman-sanctioned government. His acceptance into the now covert group added a decidedly radical tone.

Five of the original group were half brothers of Jesus or sons of Zebedee. One was his full brother by Holy Mary.

Thomas the Twin was the second and last child of Joseph and Holy Mary.[13] He remarkably resembled his older brother, Jesus; hence the name *Twin*. Thomas knew and loved Jesus as only a younger brother can. Thomas often questioned but always respected his brother. He usually participated in the back room discussions of the brave plans. While he sometimes appeared irreverent in his skepticism, he respected the wisdom of Jesus, compiling a book solely of the sayings of Jesus. This book, *The Gospel of Thomas*, provides unique insight into the philosophy of the Messiah. Thomas was twenty-five when this group of eleven men decided to do something about the problems that so concerned them.

These were the twelve men of the inner circle who set out in the year 29 C.E. to change the world as they knew it. They were the most trusted lieutenants of Jesus, and Jesus himself. Their lives intertwined with Jesus. Most abandoned family, kin and friends to pursue the dream of the New Kingdom of David. Jesus, one of the youngest, leader and conduit between God and the people, was the teacher. In matters of theology and philosophy, they seldom questioned his word. In political and military affairs, Jesus the inspirational leader delegated detailed execution to the two Peters.

Only two more entered the inner circle after they established headquarters in Capernaum. One was Matthew.[14] Matthew represented the complete outsider—tax collector, publican for Herod's government. He possessed intimate knowledge of the workings of that government. He was both an articulate speaker and a prolific writer. His father, an Essene who lived within the walls of Jerusalem, also became friendly to the cause.

The other Capernaum disciple was Mary Magdalene.[15] She joined the group to become a most devoted follower after Jesus cured her of madness. Always at the side of Jesus, she sometimes found herself shunned by male disciples.

In his thirtieth year, Jesus closed the dye shop to devote his whole being to the cause. Simon Peter and Andrew felt it would be safer for the organization to move to Capernaum. The group agreed. Five disciples called Capernaum home. They were all well-respected businessmen. The populace of the community would be receptive to their aims. Isolated by distance, terrain and temperament, the people of Capernaum felt little loyalty to either the Roman government or to the priestly authorities. Even the small Roman garrison there would prove to be trustworthy. Capernaum was a good choice.

Jesus needed to prove himself an anointed teacher before the people would accept him as leader. Only one person held the power and mystic aura to serve as the link between Jesus and the people. That person was John the Baptist, second cousin of Jesus. John the Baptist preached powerfully, a persuasive teacher holding court in a remote area near the mouth of the River Jordan and the Dead Sea. He was the son of Holy Mary's cousin, Elizabeth. Many sought him out to ease their angst over uncertain times and to shield them from apocalyptic disaster. Jesus needed his "voice in the wilderness."

Many faithful thought John the Baptist to be the promised Messiah.[16] John consistently refused the title of Messiah, but told Essene-style of the imminent coming of the one who would restore the Kingdom of God upon this Earth.

In those troubled times, multitudes came to John to be cleansed of all sin. They did this by professing repentance and belief in the single God, and by John immersing them in the River Jordan one time. John administered 'baptism' to all who would believe, but he disavowed all suggestions that he was deific, divine. Despite the public renouncements and lack of political activity, Herod and the High Priest still feared John for his power over the people.

Of course, Jesus knew John the Baptist. John's mother, Elizabeth, was not only a cousin of Holy Mary but also one her closest friends. Elizabeth's husband Zacharias instructed Mary as a youth and as High Priest of Qumran championed her to be the mother of the Messiah. Jesus was the same age as John and they came of age in the same region. John represented the religious radical: Jesus extended radicalism to cultural morés and economics. Both yearned for the return of the Kingdom of David. When Jesus sent Andrew as an emissary to John the Baptist, John was eager to cooperate.

A plan was devised. Both Jesus and his second cousin were well aware of the sensitiveness of the superstitious populace. They also realized that that very superstitiousness could be manipulated. If Jesus was to be accepted as God incarnate on earth, the Holy One appointed to be King of the New Kingdom by the single God himself, pure, more than man, born supernaturally, with all power and wisdom, it would be unseemly for a mere man, John the Baptist, to give his blessing through baptism, yet the reputation and following represented by this voice in the wilderness was essential to launch the campaign. God would have to intervene.

John prepared the believers. To the throngs that gathered along the River Jordan to hear him, he repeated a strong message: the Messiah was alive at that instant! He would present himself at one of the baptismal ceremonies. John confessed that he was not worthy to even touch the Messiah. God would actually baptize the Messiah. John would only provide the setting.

This approach neatly solved the tricky question, "How could a human, even as great and perfect as John the Baptist, give Holy Blessing to the Messiah?"

The crowd hushed as Jesus, accompanied by Andrew, approached the baptismal site. Gasps of amazement broke the silence as the purple-clad Jesus walked directly into the water where John prepared to play his role. John triumphantly raised his arms and shouted, "This is the Messiah!" The crowd broke into thunderous celebration and joyful expectation, the noise deafening, the confusion overwhelming. John later told all who would listen exactly what happened that day in the cool clear water of the River Jordan.

Jesus approached John. John lifted his arms and Jesus fell backwards as if toppled in sleep. As Jesus came up from complete immersion, the heavens opened. From the clouds came a voice which proclaimed, "This is my son, of whom I am well-pleased." Sometimes when telling the story, John added that an intense beam of light or even the image of a human-like ghost appeared among the clouds. Always he spoke of the dove.

The dove was a symbol of the poor people. It became the logo of the Davidians. As the voice spoke from the clouds, a dove descended and rested on the shoulder of Jesus. This was the dove of the people, the dove that the humble and destitute offered to the temple as redemptive sacrifices. A dove had flown from the rod of Joseph to anoint him Keeper of Mary. It was a dove that Jesus had fashioned of clay and given life. Like a dove that could rise above the filth and misery of poverty, the insurgency symbolized a movement for the poor led by the rich and privileged who could somehow always rise above their beneficiaries.

The dove, purposefully selected, appealed to the masses, the common people. Jesus would walk with the poor. He would hear their problems. He would heal their afflictions. He would cast out demons so often associated with poverty. The dove was a fitting symbol to initiate the public support-building phase of the insurgency. As the dove had shown Noah the way to land, the new life on earth after the great flood, the dove of Jesus would show the way to freedom.

Of those present at the baptism of Jesus, many had already heard stories of his virgin birth and childhood feats of magic. They came to witness and partake in the rite or one-time baptism. They each sought a new route to spiritual contentment. Little wonder that despite being unable to see or hear much of the details of the proceedings, many of the crowd perceived the miracle of the conversion of the man Jesus into an angelic holy spirit, Jesus Messiah. They wanted to believe!

Three years of propaganda, a public support-building campaign, would remove all doubts that some on the banks of the River Jordan might have had that day. As time passed, they believed more certainly that the voice of God had thundered from the clouds and that the Holy Spirit had appeared in the form of a dove. Story became truth. God, not John, had cleansed Jesus of sin and proclaimed him Messiah.

One more ritual remained for Jesus before he could teach righteousness under the law. Tradition demanded for him as for the great teacher Moses before him that he demonstrate his worth and God's favor by surviving forty days and forty nights in the dreaded wilderness.[17]

The wilderness, a near-barren desert, consisted of rock hills, deep waterless ravines, shifting sand, gravel rock gardens, salt dunes, clay cliffs spotted with salt and occasional scrub trees. Dangerous highway robbers often retreated to the safety of that poor land. Sometimes the probationer would meet another pilgrim during his forty day trial, but tradition forbade them to aid one another. The wilderness was a challenge to be faced and conquered alone.

The wilderness trial was no surprise to Jesus. He had anticipated that test from the day in the Temple at age twelve when he had proven himself worthy to be selected by the priests to become a righteous teacher. He knew that the test would be required as he approached the time in life when study, deliberation and experience would endow him with significant insight and knowledge. His grandfather Joachim and his father Joseph had completed the test, but they never told Jesus what to expect or how to survive in the wilderness. It was forbidden to tell anything of one's own experiences during the forty day test. Amazingly, disciples would later detail Jesus' trials in spite of the tradition of secrecy.

Jesus not only overcame hunger, thirst and solitude, he also overcame the Devil himself. Near the end of the forty days, Jesus was hungry and near death. His mind blurred the difference between reality and fantasy. During the day, the sun created kinescopic light patterns through the entrance of the clay cave where he lay. At night, silence and darkness played on his consciousness. The light of dreams filled sleep and dead dark the wakefulness.

On the last day, the light of morning filled the entranceway or was it the omniscient imagery of a dream? Only the daylight hours of one day remained until the test would be completed. At sundown, the fortieth day would end.

Into the dawn illumination, back-lighted by the early morning sun, stepped the evil angel, Satan. The Devil tempted Jesus to use his powers to aid himself. They both knew that this unrighteous act would do violence to the rite of forty days in the wilderness. The Devil said, "If you are the son of God, make these stones into bread so you may live."

Jesus answered, "I live not by bread, but by the word of God."

Satan then flew Jesus to a very high mountain. From that high point, they could see all the kingdoms of the world. The Devil told Jesus, "If you will kneel down and worship me, I will make you King of all you see."

Jesus refused, saying "It is written that one will worship only the single God, YHWH."

Satan then made Jesus appear on the high pinnacle of a temple steeple. He tempted Jesus to use his powers to fly down from the dangerous perch. Jesus refused. "It is written. One must not tempt God."

Sometime during that long day, Jesus passed into a totally exhausted sleep. He awoke after sunset, still in the cave. Some men who must have looked like angels to him were giving aid to revive him. They placed cold water on his forehead and gave him warm goats milk to drink. The Devil was gone.

Jesus left the wilderness and began a slow journey to Capernaum. Along the way he told of the single God and the coming of God's Kingdom on earth. He taught insights into life, death and human relationships gleaned from the wisdom of his Jewish forebears and his own powerful intellect.

Jesus knew interpretation and execution of the laws of the single God were concentrated in the hands of the religious and political few. He set out to challenge this power that had been handed down from generation to generation with only an occasional new entrant allowed. As a supposed direct descendant of King David, Jesus claimed the right to pursue the art of righteous teacher without the sanction of the Temple. Long years of study, trials and tests confirmed his readiness to teach. And, Jesus was special. He was tagged as the Messiah who would lead the people to new glory and peace.

Jesus soon found himself in the village of his youth, in Nazareth. There he planned to test his claim to the Messiahship.

Unexpected problems arose.

Nazareth, a very small place in a very rural section of Galilee, was not even noted on maps of the day. Annas, second most-high priest of all Israel and Judea, native of Nazareth, held the very powerful office of Executive of the Law. From his quarters in the Temple of Jerusalem, he dutifully exercised his authority which included harsh punishment for those found guilty of blasphemy. The citizens of Nazareth well knew this pious, vindictive old man. They feared but respected his powerful position while scorning him as a man.

Annas despised Jesus. He feared that Jesus just might be the Messiah. That would mean an end to his power. Annas had impugned Jesus since Jesus lay in Mary's womb. It was he who charged Joseph with fornication with Mary. He also charged Jesus with blasphemy for making clay doves on the Sabbath. Likely some of the tales of Jesus' youthful magic and sorcery started with Annas. Now he spread stories that Jesus was a dangerous blasphemer, hinting that associating with the pretender would mean trouble with the authorities.

When Jesus attempted to teach in his old synagogue, he was not well-received.[18] It was not time to openly announce his claim to be Messiah, but he knew that he had to *hint* of it. Among his first attempts as teacher, he read a passage from the holy text predicting the coming of the Messiah. When he finished, he raised his eyes from the scroll to utter, "I am he."

"Who are you?" someone in the small crowd yelled.

"I am he who comes from the wilderness,' Jesus carefully answered, but then dangerously added, "Is it not written?"

"You are nothing more than the little bare-footed boy who played in this very street, here by this synagogue," a young man countered.

"You were the child sorcerer," a voice from within the crowd charged. "You killed a playmate."

"I have changed," Jesus responded. "My powers will henceforth be used only to help the poor and afflicted. You will see."

A hushed buzz began in the crowd. They began to disperse until there was only one man, standing before Jesus with his eyes fixed on the ground near his feet. "John the Baptist is dead," he whispered. "Herod had him beheaded and presented his head to Salomé. You are truly the voice from the wilderness."

A tear formed in Jesus' eye. He thanked the young man for the information and left the synagogue.

Jesus admitted defeat. His home town was not the place to begin the war. He would leave Nazareth for Capernaum. A mob now gathered outside the synagogue, hastening his decision to exit the city. Perhaps the people of Capernaum would be more receptive to the word. Certainly, it would be safer. Half of the disciples of Jesus already lived in Capernaum. They could provide facilities and cover. There, he would launch a renewed start of the infant campaign. There, the most trusted twelve would be molded into the core of the insurgency.

First, though, he would have to get out of Nazareth alive.

Jesus Heals and Teaches

"And Jesus went about all the cities and villages, teaching in their synagogues, and preaching the Gospel of the Kingdom, and healing every sickness and every disease among the people."

The Holy Bible, Matthew 9:35

The crowd reassembled outside the synagogue, becoming angrier and angrier as they deciphered the message Jesus had so carefully coded.

"He claims to be the Messiah," one woman exclaimed.

"He is no more than the son of that crazy witch, Mary," another added.

"He must die," all repeated.

As Jesus attempted to leave the synagogue, the mob grabbed him and 'thrust him out of the city' and 'forced him to the crest of a hill.' From this high cliff, the crowd planned to 'cast him down headlong' to his death. A strange thing saved Jesus. In their excited frenzy, those holding Jesus released their hold and the crowd allowed Jesus to walk, untouched, to his freedom. He headed east toward friendlier climes.[1]

Within one week, the insurgents had assembled in Tiberias. In addition to Jesus, the other Nazarenes, Nathaniel Bartholomew, James the Younger, Thomas the Twin and Judas Thaddeus passed along the trail from Nazareth to the resort and fishing port of Tiberias. Judas Iscariot had renounced the Jewish authorities and abandoned his lucrative tax collector position and became an insurgent when his mentor, John the Baptist, was arrested. Since that day, he was always near Jesus. He walked away from the mob at Nazareth with Jesus and accompanied him to Tiberias. At Tiberias, the fishermen of Capernaum — Simon Peter, Andrew and Philip — appeared with a large fishing ship. The sea would soon separate the Nazarenes from an unreceptive audience.

The ship was quickly boarded and under way. Fair winds assured a fast broad reach: an overnight sail to Capernaum.

As night settled over the moonlit water, Jesus began to instruct his disciples. The lesson would not be forgotten.

Jesus stressed the importance of the propaganda role in overthrowing the government. The people would have to believe two things: the Rome-sanctioned government was contrary to God's will and a God-blessed Kingdom was imminent. If the people believed the Kingdom of God was soon to be, Jesus would accept the responsibility to convince them that he was the rightful King of the New Kingdom.

"You must become fishers of men," he declared. "You must travel the entire land, as far north as Syria, as far south as the great sands. You must preach to the people that the New

Kingdom is at hand. Do not sit back in smug, pious, self-righteous Essene style and expect the Kingdom to come to you, to you alone. The Kingdom is for all, for all those of the Twelve Tribes. There are those such as the Pharisees who have drifted from the true way, but we are all Jews. The Promised Land of God is for all Jews: for all Jews who believe.[2]

"It is not the end of the world," he continued. "It is the beginning. The Messiah is sent to rule the New Kingdom. The Scriptures will be fulfilled. The King shall sit on the right hand of God and rule over this promised land — this land that shall be holy!"[3]

"The people will come to believe. Their expectations will be great. The power and the will of the people must be so strong that those corrupt, evil priests will fall in their own filth. A government that does not obey the will of the people and uphold the law of God shall not long stand. When the Herod government falls, our Roman exploiters will leave. They will not have the military strength to enslave every Israelite when they have lost their collaborators. With the people on our side, we shall prevail.

Jesus remonstrated his lieutenants. "We must build our campaign upon a solid foundation. Like he who digs deep in order to build his house upon firm bedrock, we must build the Kingdom upon the deep, solid faith of the people."[4]

The sun shone high overhead when the fishing ship drifted into home port. About two dozen people, filled with expectation, met the vessel slipping quietly into a protected cove. They had been told of Jesus by the fishermen of Capernaum.

Jesus wasted little time before digging the foundation of the cause. The next morning, he lingered in the street near the synagogue of Capernaum, holding court as a healing physician.[5]

His good works would be the bedrock upon which the new world would emerge. This little bald-headed man, sitting on a stone fence in a small fishing village of assorted unmatched huts oddly placed on the windward shore of the Sea of Galilee, nurtured the foundation of a massive rebellion. A single, yet strong, foundation it was: the perception that one man was empowered by God to heal and drive out demons.

A large, unkempt dirty man approached Jesus. An unearthly voice issued from his seemingly unwilling mouth. He uttered "Help me" in his own voice but the demon overpowered the pitiful cry. In a horrible, shrill voice, the demon wailed, "Let us alone, Jesus of Nazareth. Why would you destroy us of Capernaum? You, who claim to be the Holy One of God, will surely bring the authorities to persecute us. You must leave."

Jesus looked directly at the poor man and commanded the unclean spirit by name to leave the man's body. There ensued a terrible screeching sound, the man's body tore open, a black glob poured out, formed a recognizable demon, and flew away.[6]

The story of Jesus casting out the demon circulated throughout the region. No one seemed to know the possessed man nor could any remember just what the demon looked like. They all agreed, however, that a dirty, mean-spirited man had hurled insults at Jesus, suddenly became passive and quiet and calmly walked away. Witnesses notwithstanding, word spread that Jesus of Nazareth could cast out demons.

Jesus remained in Capernaum for several months, a time to consolidate his base of power and develop a coherent philosophy upon which the New Kingdom would be ruled.[7] He was a Jew. As such, he would not abandon the teaching of his forbears in which he was well-versed. He would, as Messiah, reinterpret parts of the law.

He modified strict adherence to the Sabbath,[8] adopted the Roman calendar,[9] and damned the function of the money lender that both diaspora and Temple Jews were assuming in trade and commerce.[10] These were rules concerning economics in a time that trade and inter-relationships among various cultures were very important.

To the faithful, Jesus' most sweeping changes were to modify harsh, patriarchal laws of personal conduct to a much more human system. He did not intend to change or rewrite the Scriptures. He would only teach what God had intended when it inspired ancients to write the law. Thus, Jesus assumed powers not normally granted a rabbi and assured conflict with the priestly authorities who had sole sanction to interpret and enforce the law. He knew a clash was inevitable.

Every Holy Day, Jesus taught in the synagogue. He taught that mental processes could be just as damning as physical acts. "If you insult your brother, you shall be brought before the council of law. You must love your brother as you love yourself." Jesus said of the importance of love within the Jewish family. "But," he continued, "if you, in anger, call your brother a fool, your sacrifice gift will not be accepted and you may burn in hell, until you reconcile."[11]

"Any man who looks at a woman with sexual desire in his heart has already committed adultery," he stated.[12]

Jesus changed the old Jewish law that permitted a husband to divorce his wife without cause, saying "Whosoever gives notice of divorce to his wife for any reason except fornication has not divorced her. If she remarries, both she and her lover commit adultery and shall be punished accordingly."[13]

One cruel and ancient law Jesus did not change. If a married woman committed adultery or an unmarried woman was found with child, death by stoning was required. The unborn child would, of course, die in the mother's womb. In at least one case, Jesus did show compassion for a woman that was about to be stoned, but he did not change the law.

"A man's personal word is his oath. A man must not swear to tell the truth by God, earth or Jerusalem. Nor shall he affirm that he will tell the truth. When a Jew answers yes, it is yes. When he answers no, it is no. Anything else is wrong and evil."[14]

Jesus taught the often unheeded virtue of refraining from retaliation for a supposed insult, transgression, theft or physical injury.[15] He commanded his listeners to lend money with no interest return expected (and never to place money in a bank).[16] He said all humans should love one another.[17]

Jesus said, "Give freely to those in need. Give because of your love of mankind, not so people will praise you for your generosity."[18]

He taught, "Fast for God, not for man. Fast in such a manner that only you and God know you sacrifice."[19]

"It is a sin to eat or drink more than your body needs to sustain life.[20] Do not hoard and accumulate wealth. Refuse to be a slave to materialism.[21] Serve only the single God. Always look at the bright side of life. Do not judge the actions of others. Keep prayer between yourself and God. Do not use prayer to announce to others your wishes and beliefs.[22] Be humble in deed, sure in appearance. Do not proclaim your supposed righteousness. God sees the truly devout, and few they are. Above all things, do to others what you would like them to do to you.[23] This is the law as the prophets meant it to be. This is the law as it should have been transcribed." All this, Jesus taught.

He confidently quoted the Torah concerning his own status, "Beware of false prophets who come to you in sheep's clothing, but inwardly they are ravening wolves."[24] He warned his listeners that not all those who would teach the law were sanctioned by God. He thus hinted that the evil priestly authorities were false prophets and his word was true. He would soon prove his worth by a series of humanitarian accomplishments.

Jews during the time of Jesus believed that all human sickness was caused by evil spirits. These spirits usually lived within the body of the sick person. This possession was more apparent in cases of dementia than in cases of physical injury, but the evil spirit was present in all pain. The evil spirit or demon seemed much more comfortable occupying a person who had slipped from the faith. The task of the physician or magician now became the identification of the demon by name and the exorcism from the sick person. In success, the demon would leave the body of the inflicted person and search for a more comfortable habitation. Jesus was a master of exorcism.

Simon Peter and Andrew came to the synagogue very sad and grieved. Their mother-in-law fell sick with a high fever. Jesus went to her house and approached the sick bed. The fever immediately subsided and she followed her motherly instinct and helped comfort those who cried for her.[25]

The house was near the fishing dock. At the door, a crowd asked Jesus for help. Jesus followed the crowd to the fishing dock where two divers suffered from the bends. He called the devils possessing the divers by name and commanded them to leave silently. The healed divers and the crowd were amazed.[26]

A leper approached Jesus. The crowd, fearing contamination, moved to open a path. Jesus, filled with compassion, reached out his hand to touch the leper. The crowd gasped in horror. Jesus simply said, "Be clean" and the leprosy left the man. Then Jesus sent the grateful man away, adding, "Show your self to the priests."[27] The priests would understand that their positions of authority were endangered.

The ruling priests' awareness of Jesus' following forced him to operate more covertly in the mostly rural areas. That was part of the plan.[28]

Within a few weeks, Jesus and his disciples had recruited and trained seventy new disciples in Capernaum. These seventy fanned out throughout the would-be New Kingdom to spread the word that an insurrection was soon to occur — an insurrection led by the righteous teacher Jesus — an insurrection that would result in a God-directed kingdom as existed under David.[29]

With Capernaum as a central base, Jesus began to expand the campaign to win the hearts and minds of the populace into the countryside. Sometimes the disciples would accompany him. Always a curious crowd followed.

His first recorded stop was at a wedding in Cana. At the wedding, Jesus demonstrated the ability to perform another sort of miracle, exorcising greed from men's hearts.[30]

Mary, Mother of Jesus, had responsibility for the wedding festivities at Cana. The entire town turned out to drink, eat and celebrate the marriage. As the evening wore on, the wine jugs emptied, and Mary asked Jesus what she should do. Jesus instructed the servants to fill the wine jugs to the brim with water. The slaves continued to serve from the jugs and the gluttonous party continued. The water from the jugs tasted so good that the mayor of the town complimented the bridegroom on 'the fine old wine.' The disciples were amazed.

After the party, word passed to Jesus that a high-ranking Roman military officer had summoned him back to Capernaum. Jesus was surprised to learn that the Centurion was a convert to the truth of the single God and had actually built a synagogue for his Jewish faith brothers. A benefactor with such faith and power could not be ignored.[31]

Compelled to change his plans for a few days, Jesus returned to Capernaum. He could remain there only a short time lest the authorities receive word and order him and the disciples arrested. An entourage consisting of Jesus, his mother, his disciples, all his remaining brothers and sisters and some curious followers made the thirty mile hike around the north side of the Sea of Galilee to the new fishing village.

The Roman officer humbled himself before Jesus when Jesus entered the large home. "I am not worthy that you should enter my home," the Centurion remarked. "But please, heal my beloved servant who now lies on his deathbed."

Jesus was surprised. This Roman put himself in grave danger to approach a prelect —public teacher of the single God — for help! Jesus thanked the soldier for his faith and support. As he turned to leave, the slave appeared, healthy and able, at the top of the stairs.

Jesus attempted to rest in the house of a friend before he again left Capernaum. A large crowd gathered outside and pushed against the door until it burst open. Four men pushed through the crowd, thick with the curious and the believers. Above their heads they carried a friend, very sick with the palsy, on a small cot. Jesus sensed that there were scribes, translators of the law, studying him from the mob. He could not shrink from duty. He spoke to the sick man, "You have sinned. Because I am the Son of Man, I could forgive you of your sins, or I could command you to rise and be well. Either way, your illness would be cured because you would be free of sin."[32]

The man smiled. Jesus held his hands high so that all could see, and said in a loud voice that all could hear, "I command you, rise up and carry your bed." The man rose up and exited through the excited crowd.

That night, Jesus and his disciples tried to eat and drink. Many non-believing Roman relatives of the Centurion, tax collectors and minor government bureaucrats now occupied the large room — they too taking supper. Some of the pious Pharisees rebuked Jesus for eating with the outsiders, but Jesus said to them, "I have come not for the truly righteous, but to save the sinners."[33]

Next morning, Jesus and his disciples attempted to make their way from the house to the waiting fishing ship. A multitude of people packed around them, impeding their progress. Along the way, they passed the open office door of Matthew Levi, a customs collector and son of Alphaeus. Jesus asked him to join them as a disciple. Without hesitating, Matthew Levi closed the office door and followed Jesus.[34] Now there were twelve lieutenants in the closely knit inner core of the insurgency. Only one more would join — a woman: Mary Magdalene.

At the seaside, Jesus' mother and some brothers and sisters attempted to break through the crowd to see him. When told of them, Jesus said he did not wish to see them. "Those people out there are my true family. Whoever serves God is my brother, sister and mother."[35]

The crowd pressed against Jesus and the disciples. With difficulty, they slowly progressed down the beach. The ship awaited them in the cove, tied to the rickety dock jutting out into the water. Within half an hour, the ship got underway with its load of aspiring revolutionaries.

Simon Peter, the captain, advised against attempting a crossing of the Sea of Galilee. A storm approached from the west. Attempting passage into the storm would be unpredictable and dangerous. Jesus decided to anchor near the shore of a remote isolated area about five miles southeast of Capernaum.

They had trouble approaching the windward shore. As the ship touched bottom. Andrew dropped anchor. It bit deep. Firmly anchored, the ship retreated from shore as the crew let out anchor line.

Jesus and part of the crew crawled over the gunnel to half swim, half walk ashore, there, they hoped to find provisions to ride out the storm. Their reconnoiter ended unsuccessfully.[36]

"This place is a desert," shouted Mark from the vantage point of a high dune. "There are no farm animals, no people. We're stuck on an isolated desert by the sea."

Luke joined Mark on the high dune. "Look," he exclaimed. "The multitude is coming down the beach. They have followed us."

Soon five thousand people crowded around Jesus, asking him to teach them. Some sought to be healed. All hoped to share the wisdom and knowledge of the master righteous teacher.

Jesus was delighted. He felt compassion for these people who followed aimlessly like unshepherded sheep. He would teach them. He would be their good shepherd who would show them the way to good and right.[37] Enough sheep could overwhelm an unholy government.

Jesus taught and held court until late into the night. He slept fitfully that short night. The excitement of the occasion, the howling wind, a dark sky electrified by lightning made for restless repose for the others. Morning was slow to dawn for them.

Excited disciples shook the sluggish Jesus. "We must leave," they insisted. "The authorities will soon find us. The ship is bouncing on the bottom. It will soon be fast aground."

Jesus slowly arose, walked to a pool of water in the sand, scooped the clear liquid in his cupped hands and washed his face and head. He asked, "What do the people eat"

"Nothing," admitted the disciples.

"Nothing."

"We have nothing to feed the people."

"Only five loaves of bread and two fish for five thousand people," the dispirited Jude declared, clarifying the situation. "There is no town, no place to buy bread. We have word the authorities are near. We must leave at once to take our chances in the storm."

Jesus surveyed the multitude. They were so innocent, so like little children full of faith in him and the cause. He felt love and responsibility for them. Was he not their shepherd? They must not remain hungry. He walked into the middle of them, barking orders like a seasoned centurion. "You and you. Divide this group into hundreds. You, group the followers into formations. On line. Look sharp!"

Some of the five thousand formed into *companies* of fifties, *centuries* of one hundreds, and *cohorts* of five hundred. They formed a huge crescent around their commander.

Jesus spoke to the military-like formation. "You are the vanguard of the New Kingdom. Upon you I place the trust of solidarity of the northern shore. Admit nothing to the authorities, but recruit your family and close friends to await the day of judgment. You and yours will inherit the New Kingdom."

Jesus then turned to his lieutenants and commanded, "Feed them."

The five loaves and two fish were pushed among the ranks. No one ate and all were filled. They learned a lesson in selflessness that day.[38]

An extremely strong low atmospheric pressure area to the west of Capernaum caused a strong cyclonic wind. The water of the Sea of Galilee dropped, blown toward the low pressure area. The ship, anchored about three-quarters of a mile offshore, soon rested high and dry on the bottom of the sea.

The disciples that had remained on the ship wondered what to do next. The ship's crew could not row a dinghy against a wind to pick them up. Their concern soon departed. Jesus, the new disciple Matthew Levi and the remaining land party walked across the hard-packed bottom toward the ship. Jesus found a shoaled path and appeared to walk on water to the ship. The others followed. All climbed aboard to await a change in tide. They did not wait long.[39]

A wall of water approached the vessel. The huge wave lifted the small ship, threw it toward shore and pushed it back out to deep water by backwash.

The crew quickly hoisted shortened sail. The wind shifted to the south. Gale winds continued. Water washed over the deck. Rain fell in sharp, piercing torrents.

Jesus walked across the pitching deck. He looked seaward over the bow as if commanding the storm to still. Suddenly it did. There was an eerie quiet. The water was flat and still. Only an occasional patch of white foam hinted of the storm.[40]

Then, as suddenly as it stopped, the wind returned, this time from the east. The shortened sail handled the run well. The crisis was over. They made landfall at Gennesaret about two miles from Mafala and five miles north of the destination, Tiberias. Simon Peter and Andrew would later sail the ship to the port at Magdala before returning to Capernaum.

The people at Gennesaret had already heard of the powers of Jesus. They brought many sick — some on death beds — to be healed. Jesus gladly complied, but the more he healed, the more came. The remaining contingent soon felt compelled to move out. But everywhere they traveled, people flocked to join them and see Jesus.[41]

Jesus led his students southward out of Tiberias. This was his definitive campaign to recruit common people throughout Galilee, Samaria and Judea to the cause. They traveled, mostly on foot, through Scythopolis, Adamah, Jericho, touching Bethany and Jerusalem before returning north. During the three month tour, they taught the philosophy of Jesus and imminence of the Kingdom of God. Always, Jesus was the intellectual and spiritual core upon which all hope was based. Jesus as a healer attracted the people and his teachings recruited them. There was no fear. The teaching was clear and direct. The call to arms was unmistakable.

Walking along the road, Jesus and the disciples pulled bread from their bags to eat. Some pious Pharisee reminded Jesus that Jewish law forbade eating with unwashed hands. Jesus first chastised the Pharisees for that sect's tradition of ignoring two other laws. Then he proclaimed the law requiring clean hands to be void. He reasoned, "It is that which comes from a man's heart that can defile, not that which passes through his stomach."[42]

Beside the road that followed the coast of the Sea of Galilee, Jesus healed many people. There he met a deaf and dumb man. Jesus cupped his hands over the man's ears, looked to heaven, and called the demon possessing the man by name. "*Ephphtha*, I command you to leave this poor soul's body." The man spoke and heard. Farther down the road, Jesus healed a blind man by spitting in his eyes. Jesus approached a man suffering greatly from dementia. When Jesus shouted at the devils within, they left the man's body and entered some hogs.[43]

A rich rabbi begged Jesus to save his dying daughter. When the rabbi led Jesus to his home, they found the daughter dead and the women of the house wailing over her body. The women laughed when Jesus said the daughter was not dead. The spirit of life then re-entered the girl's body and she arose from the bed. Another valuable recruit for the cause was assured.[44]

Near Mt. Tabor, Jesus and his lieutenants escaped the mob of followers and the curious. Jesus needed a private audience with those who would guide the insurrection. It was a most intimate experience.[45]

He asked who they thought he was. Peter answered, "The Messiah of God."

"Yes." Jesus replied, "but there are certain events that must occur before the people will fully believe and accept me as their king. It is said that the Son of Man must suffer on a tree, be rejected by the ruling theocracy, be executed and rise from death on the third day to be King of the New Kingdom. We must fulfill these prophecies soon. You shall see the Kingdom of God before you die."

Jesus charged his lieutenants to complete loyalty in himself and the cause. "You must deny all material things, carry the crossed sword of a soldier and pledge your lives to me. You must defend all that I teach. Be ashamed of nothing. If you do these things, you will be part of the Kingdom of God."

Later that evening, he guided Simon Peter, John and James up the side of the mountain. As darkness approached, they rested in a protective depression cut into the rock slope. In a very small bronze cup, they placed a precious product of the eastern trade route — a specialty of Tyre and Sidon. After igniting a small fire, they burned the sweet-smelling powder. All held their heads near the smoke in order to breathe the mind-altering fumes. A warm sensation embraced each. A brilliant mist glowing orange and red engulfed them. They felt a deep sense of brotherly love and comradeship. Perhaps they slept. Perhaps they ascended into a beautiful, more perfect world.

Ghosts of Moses and Elijah appeared out of the mist. Jesus stood beside the two ancients. His purple robe glowed — eerie incandescent fingers of light bounced from it. It was the same voice heard at the baptism of Jesus. It spoke the same words. "This is my beloved son in whom I am well-pleased." It then added, "Listen to him."

When the three disciples awoke, the sun was announcing the birth of a new day. Jesus warned them to tell no one of the visions. The group descended from the mountain and rejoined the multitude which was camped alongside the road, eagerly awaiting their return. Jesus taught the multitude.

Jesus allowed most ancient laws to remain unchanged; much of what he taught was revolutionary.[46] While accepting most of the often harsh laws sanctioned since Moses' time, he modified some and clarified others. His interpretations harked back to a simpler more pastoral time. He sometimes instructed in parables, puzzles intended to bring out insight from within the student. He often spoke in direct forceful statements of fact. Always, his reputation as an exorcist lent credence to his teachings.

The people understood that which Jesus taught would be law in the New Kingdom. His teachings often rejected the effects of trade and commercialism that supposedly had been brought on by Roman control. The New Kingdom of David would be free of the materialism that Jesus saw all around him. Love and interdependence would provide the basics of life and rule the New Kingdom.

The landed peasant saw and understood this philosophy. Many others engaged in trade did not. Jesus made it clear that only those who would accept his precepts would be welcome in the New Kingdom.

For the contemporary of Jesus, many specific laws commanded by the teacher and rightful king were troubling. The Essenes, in particular, were shocked at their creation's liberal interpretations of the law and his teaching of love and forgiveness. But Essene leadership did not withdraw support. Instead, they watched and waited while the foundations of a new sect became clear.

The sect that was to become the Kingdom was based on the teachings of Jesus.[47] Jesus would be King. He would answer only to God. Each disciple would rule one of the twelve tribes as a direct subordinate of Jesus. All judges would be ordained by God as observed by the disciple-ruler of the tribe. Lawsuits, grievances against one's neighbors and questions of law that were normally brought before a priestly authority would not be possible for those who followed the teachings Jesus. If a person were sued, he should pay his antagonist double without a trial. Of course, no one could swear to God or even affirm to tell the truth in a court of law. A person would be required to freely loan anything asked of him. Personal property as it was then known would no longer exist. Interest could never be charged on money loaned. Gifts should be given in secret. Divorce for anything except adulterous fornication would not be sanctioned. No matter how wronged a citizen of the New Kingdom might perceive himself, even to the point of personal injury, retaliation was forbidden. A person accepting work for hire would be commanded to accept whatever pay was offered to him. Money, a symbol of value created by an earthly government, could never be used in commerce.[48] The New Kingdom would be as heaven on earth where everybody shared freely and loved one another.

Jesus often reminded listeners that persons of wealth had little chance of enjoying the coming Kingdom. He sometimes urged rich people to give all their possessions to the poor or his campaign before joining the sect. Jesus made it clear what the costs would be to enter the New Kingdom, which seemingly would massively redistribute the wealth to assure a common level of well-being.

Jesus was able to establish himself as the champion of the poor even though he himself was born of a a royal family. He knew that he had to make a strong appeal to the poor. Popular support was essential for the overthrow of a government of the privileged. He preached that the rich could never be righteous in the eyes of God even while he accepted money, supplies, lavish dinners and lodging from the upper class. He taught love, while preparing for war. The poor would rule over the rich in his kingdom.

Jesus added a surprising element to his teaching: the complete rejection of family. For Jesus, the greater community welded together by common interests and beliefs replaced the core family. The single God became so central to his philosophy that it was the father of every human. At the instant of birth, the earthly father became irrelevant; the extended community and God would provide for the baby's sustenance. When a person came of age, that person became brother or sister to all believers and the natural mother was no longer needed or wanted.[49]

All this suggested what the Jewish world would be like under Jesus. All this helped set the stage for the overthrow of a government directed by the precepts and interpretations of the Pharisee sect. Jesus taught whenever and wherever he could. Before his first visit to Jerusalem as an insurrection leader, public support for the movement had begun to spread throughout the countryside.

The first year of the campaign had been successful but much work remained before public support would reach the level necessary for the small core of insiders to overthrow the government and expel the Romans. The seventy disciples that Jesus had selected in Capernaum were already busy organizing support cells within villages and hamlets throughout the countryside. These cells would insure the survival of the insurgency core which was coming under increasing pressure from the government authorities and Roman cohorts.

Jesus and his immediate lieutenants had returned to Capernaum for only a short time when another trip to Jerusalem was planned. The insurgency needed to consolidate various rebel elements into a more unified command structure that ultimately reported to Jesus. The trip to Jerusalem was a dangerous and yet essential venture. All contacts would be, as far as possible, made in secret.

The Conspiracy Widens

"Say not ye, there are yet four months, and then cometh harvest? Behold, I say unto you, lift up your eyes and look on the fields, for they are white already to harvest."

The Hoy Bible, John 4:35

Only a handful of the inner circle departed Capernaum with Jesus. Among the disciples to make the mission with Jesus were Luke and the newest lieutenant, Matthew. Certainly, as treasurer, Judas Iscariot was included—part of the purpose of this trip was to solicit funds. Simon Zelotes, another essential member, could identify trustworthy Zealots—the second objective of the mission entailed organizing a chain of co-conspirators to help overthrow the present governments.

Thomas the Twin wanted to go with his brother but Jesus conceived a plan to send him on a diversionary expedition. Thomas so much resembled his brother that conflicting reports of the whereabouts of the Messiah were bound to surface if they went separate ways. This would confuse the Romans. Thomas went north and Jesus went south.[1]

Thomas and a small entourage of armed guards thundered out of Capernaum in the cool, early dawn. Thomas wore a conspicuous true purple robe. Simon Peter the Rock rode alongside Thomas, his garb suggesting that of a Roman officer. Andrew, also wearing military gear, followed close behind. Four slaves leading pack animals completed the caravan. The eager camels quickly transported their riders out of sight. The cloud of dust soon settled to earth. All was quiet as the sun peeked over the eastern mountains.

Jesus led his small group out of the unwalled city in the middle of the same hot morning. The citizens of Capernaum had already completed their early morning outdoor chores, drawing water and finishing breakfast. Most men already left the city to work in the surrounding fields or to cast nets into the sea (shortly after dinner). The women were for the most part busy within the walls of the small rock houses. Few noticed the group dressed in the coarse cloth robes of the poor leaving by foot along the shore highway toward Magdala. Those that did see the group did not associate such raggedy travelers with the proud Davidians.

The caravan led by Thomas and Peter the Rock stopped for the evening at an inn in the mountain way-station town of Gischala. Local residents noticed the purple-clad Thomas and asked to receive wise words and blessings from the Messiah. Brother Thomas begged that he be left unmolested to rest from a long day. No politics or religion was heard. Every member of the caravan soon fell fast asleep.

Early the next morning, the Davidians began the second half of their sixty mile journey to Tyre. The road soon topped the last mountain ridge to begin an almost constant down-slope to the port city.

At Tyre, Thomas and Peter met the African trader known as Simon of Cyrene.[2] Simon gladly accepted the symbols of value bearing the likeness of Roman Caesar Tiberius in exchange for his wares. Five fine horses, some oil that would emit dense smoke when set afire and some short Roman swords were offered, but the one treasure the Davidians most sought was a one gallon *cruse* of *silphium laciniatum*. With the trades completed, the travelers from Galilee prepared for a two day trek to Capernaum, but first they would rest for the night.

Thomas had no wish to act as a healer or wise philosopher but events gave him no choice. A people called Canaanite were the original inhabitants of the region including most of the lands now claimed—in the name of God, of course—by the Israelites. They had centuries earlier been defeated by the Israelite tribe of Asher, the tribe of Jesus' father Joseph. Their last defeat had been in the rugged mountains of northern Galilee and southern Phoenicia. Peter the Rock was certainly surprised when a woman bearing the distinctive characteristics of a Canaanite approach him for help.[3] He directed the woman to Thomas. "That man," he told her, "is surely the Messiah, descendant of David and true ruler of all Canaan."

The woman had heard stories of the great healing powers of the man who claimed to be the Messiah. Her need exceeded her pride. As Peter watched in amusement, the woman ran to Thomas and dropped to her knees. "Have mercy on me, Lord of Canaan, Son of David. You must exorcise the Devil from my grievously ill daughter."

Thomas was speechless, but as some of the entourage pulled the pleading woman away, he assumed the role of the physician/Messiah and commanded them to release her. "I am not sent only to administer to the needs of Jews. This woman is part of my flock. I will rule over Gentiles as well as Jews. She has shown faith in me. I will help her." He explained with wisdom and insight that would make the true Messiah proud that "...the Canaanites are as dogs around the table of their Jewish masters, but even dogs eat the crumbs from their master's table." The woman could in the humbled manner of a dog receive the benefit of the power of the single God.

Thomas, acting as Jesus, said to the woman, "Your faith is great. It will be as you wish. Return to your daughter. You will find her well and happy at this very moment. The Devil is gone! Your belief overcomes all!" Thus, Thomas drove the evil spirit out of the woman's daughter *in absentia*.

Thomas quickly assembled the caravan and ordered it underway back to Capernaum. He did not wish to be forced to assume the role of the Messiah of the Jews in this foreign place. The real Pretender, Jesus, also attempted to avoid notice as his small group walked into Magdala but the distress of a beautiful young woman made him take a chance.

In Magdala, Jesus did not make the traditional contact with the Essene host. Instead, he and his lieutenants accepted the invitation of the community leader of the Pharisee sect who presented a fine meal of roast lamb and old wine. The disciples—Luke, Matthew, Judas Iscariot and Simon Zelotes— seemed uneasy with the Pharisee's hospitality. Jesus reminded them that the New Kingdom was for all Jews of the Twelve Tribes. The Pharisee would change their ways once they understood the truth of his teaching.

Attracted by the fragrance of the food and the noise, a beautiful woman of the street walked through the open door to the dining area. She quickly sensed that Jesus, though still clad in peasant cloth, was special. She stood before Jesus and looked down at him on the dining couch, her feet planted apart, her back rigid, arms crossed under her breasts, chin high. She radiated dignity despite her unkempt coarse hair and dirty dark face. She smiled faintly, whispering, "I am possessed with seven demons."[4]

"You are Mary, Mary Magdalene," Jesus surmised, "you have been married many times. You seek happiness but do not find it."

"And you are a Magus to know these things. I have told no one in this city these secrets."

"Whatever I am, you shall be my disciple and follow me. You are now free of the seven devils. Your body is no longer troubled."

She felt clean and free for the first time in her memory. She dropped down upon her knees and cried in gratitude to Jesus.

She opened a small box of expensive aloe ointment and soothed the feet of Jesus with it. The cream mixed with her tears. She wiped his feet with her long hair. She kissed his feet and slowly moved to his upper body. He rolled toward her and she gently kissed his lips.

The pious Pharisee host was indignant. "Don't you know that this woman is a sinner, a whore? Why would you, supposed to be a prophet and wise teacher, allow her to touch you in this manner?"

Jesus called the Pharisee by name, "Simon, I can give this woman more than I can give you. She has sinned much, you little. Leave her. She shall sin no more."

Jesus then turned to Mary Magdalene crying on the floor. "Rise. Your sins are forgiven. Go in peace. I do not lust for you."

Many women would follow Jesus and the select twelve as they traveled from city to city, village to village. Joanna, wife of Herod's personal steward, Chuza, Susanna and many more gave Jesus their "substance."[5] Mary Magdalene proved to be one of the most faithful and loving of all his disciples but she and Jesus never had sex together.

The travelers did not choose (as might be expected) the road along the Sea of Galilee from Magdala to Tiberias and down the valley formed by the River Jericho. The route from Jericho to Jerusalem was easiest and most-traveled. Instead, they left Magdala, heading westward for a short distance, then turning south. They passed Mt. Tabor, crossed the plain of Esdraelon and climbed the mountain divide leading southward through the small cities of Ginea and Samaria. Neither seeking food nor lodging from the local inhabitants along the way, they ate *manna*[6] and slept outside in the cold night air. At Bethel, just a few miles north of Jerusalem, they made a most important contact.

Joseph of Arimathea was a well-known and respected businessman and political leader. He was also a member of the Council of High Priests, the Sanhedrin, who ruled on all matters of law. Simon Zelote knew Joseph well as a friend and comrade-in arms. They were both active Zealot insurgents.

Arimathea, Joseph's private estate, lay just west of Bethel. His principal residence perched high on a rock mesa, a defensible position in case of attack. Joseph led the travelers to the foot of a long stairwell cut from the sheer rock face. There servants helped them cleanse and change robes. A ritual feast followed.

"Sons of God," spoke the host, holding his wine cup high with his right hand as he leaned on his left arm, "to our victory and the return of the Kingdom of David."

Each participant knew the road would be long and dangerous as they held their cups in salute to the host.

Jesus rose to speak. "You, my comrades, have given much for the Kingdom. I say to you, anyone who will not give up his wife, family and home and take up the sword and follow me is not worthy of the Kingdom. Before victory is ours, brother shall fight brother, father shall leave his family to become part of the cause, and mother shall give her milk to sustain the life of the enemy.[7]

The men's communion lasted well into the night. During that time, Jesus spoke to Joseph and detailed plans for the overthrow. It was essential for Joseph to remain in his position of trust in the Temple. He would be a critical key to victory.

At dawn, the diners still slept soundly on the dining couches. Sunlight streamed into the large open room, slowly awakening the men to the new day. The intellectual discourse, plentiful food and good wine had already welded bonds of comradeship. Arimathea, the place, would be lost into dust but retain a place in memory for thousands of years.[8]

The weary, drug-weakened travelers stumbled into Jerusalem early that evening. Guided by Simon Zelote, they made their way through the northern section of the city to what was called the Essene quarter. Their destination was a comfortable three story residence, wedged between smaller homes along a narrow back street, the house that belonged to the father of John Mark Eutychus—Zealot.[9]

Simon Zelote was very familiar with the dwelling that oddly rose twenty feet above its neighbors. The open third floor, called the upper room, served as a central meeting place for Zealot insurgents. The Marks, uncircumcised Gentiles, found themselves shunned by righteous Essene Jews who dominated the quarter. Their home, avoided by the general population, offered relatively safe haven for religious and political deviants. A quick turn off the busy street though a dark door and up the narrow stairway put the pedestrian into another world —a world of conspiracy and hope.

Jesus and his lieutenants remained in Jerusalem for several weeks. Most of this time Jesus remained in the Mark house teaching those carefully selected for trustworthiness. All who were now included in the Davidian movement agreed that a citizen named Nicodemus had to be recruited for their cause.[10] Nicodemus served as an officer of the Temple police—his assignment: commander of the Temple Guard. This position placed him in an intimate relationship with the inner working of the council. On the day of accounting, when the Messiah would return from the dead to assume his rightful place as King, having the Temple police on the right side would be most helpful!

Simon Zelote trusted this Pharisee Nicodemus, who, even though a Pharisee sect member, in secret meetings had shown great sympathy for the Zealot cause. Nicodemus demonstrated his commitment to the Zealot cause by killing a priest-judge selected by the Zealot underground. A central objective of the covert trip now underway was to convince Nicodemus that the best instrument to overthrow the current government was Jesus and the Davidian organization.

Several night meetings between Jesus and Nicodemus were scheduled at the home of John Mark's father. Nicodemus soon came to admire the wisdom of Jesus while Jesus respected the open-minded reception the Pharisees extended to Jesus.

Nicodemus did proclaim his belief in the power of Jesus. "Rabbi, I know that you are a teacher inspired by God. I know of the healing miracles you have performed. No man could work without the help of God, but I have my Pharisee beliefs ingrained since my birth. How, I ask you, can I discard those ideals and accept your arguments?"

"You must be born again. You must start with a blank mind and relearn all that you have been taught. Unless you can do that, you cannot be part of the Kingdom of God."

Nicodemus, confused, replied, "How can I do that? How can a grown man reenter his mother's womb and be born again?"

Jesus explained, "You are two parts: one is flesh and blood and the other is your essence—your spirit. The spirit is like the wind; it is there, but you cannot see it. It is your spirit that must die and be reborn again."

Nicodemus questioned further. "How can these things be?"

Jesus answered, "You must accept all as does a child, without reason, with complete faith."[11]

The teaching and learning sessions continued for many nights. As time passed, Nicodemus came to understand how the spiritual things could be. He came to believe that only Jesus could emerge from the chaos of a revolution as leader of Israel and Judea. Only a wise man of God, inspired—born—of God could lead a Godly nation back to the glory of the Kingdom of David.

One night Jesus issued a strange statement. "I have told you of earthly things. If you do not believe those, how can I teach you of heavenly things? No human can ascend up to heaven. Only those who come from heaven can return. For that reason, God gave his son to teach mortal man how to live forever on earth. Only those who believe me will live. All others will die. My knowledge and understanding is the light of the world."[12]

Nicodemus did not fully understand but he was truly under the hypnotic power of Jesus' intellect. He would prove to be one of the most loyal and certainly one of the most important Davidian insurgents.

Jesus met through introduction other Zealots in and around Jerusalem. Most came to him in the upper room, accompanied by Simon Zelote, Nicodemus and the father of John Mark. One was of such importance that Jesus would visit him. Young and very rich, a committed Zealot, converted to the Essene faith, he carried the name John Mark.

An elegant host, young John Mark Eutychus greeted Jesus, Luke and Simon Zelote at the courtyard bath of his spacious cut-rock home in the nearby village of Bethany. He participated in the ritual cleansing of his guests in preparation for the communal meal called agape. The Mount of Olives could be seen from the rear courtyard of the John Mark home while the front entrance yard faced the main village square.

Another guest, Simon Magus, blessed the bread, the new wine and the fruits. Simon Magus carried the reputation as a magician of some repute. Jesus, upset that Simon Magus would be afforded the honor of acting Prince of Israel, realized that his message had not yet fully reached Bethany.

That night John Mark and his sisters Mary and Martha came to believe that Jesus offered the only real hope for the establishment of the Kingdom of David. Simon Magus would no longer be extended the head honor in their house. However, Simon Magus continued to be a mystical leader and devotee of the insurgent cause, if not of Jesus.

The agape did not include the overtly sexual acts that would much later come to be associated with some sects of Jesus followers. Instead, they consumed much bread and wine in symbolic salutes to God and the cause.

As the wine flowed and inhibitions loosened, Jesus bonded in friendship with John Mark, Mary and Martha, remaining several days in their hospitality. During that time, the three rich and important citizens of Bethany became dedicated champions for Jesus as Messiah.

After returning to Jerusalem, Jesus committed what nearly proved to be for both him and the insurgency a fatal mistake. He allowed his emotions to overpower reason.

As Passover approached, pilgrims filled the streets of Jerusalem. Jesus and his disciples left the home of John Mark's father and ventured onto the Temple grounds.

What Jesus saw in the Temple incensed him. Vendor booths promoted the joys of all aspects of materialism. Some exchanged Temple coins for money accepted only by Roman occupiers. Others loaned money at interest. Some sold imported rugs and drugs. Several sold doves and animals to be offered as sacrifices at the nearby altar.

Jesus made a whip and began to lash out at vendors. He overturned tables. Coins and precious jewelry scattered onto the stone walkway. Someone in the crown grabbed him and restrained him. Still, he shouted furiously, "You cannot kill me." He pounded his chest to indicate the immortality of his body. "Take this Temple, this life, and in three days it will return."[13]

With the help of some pilgrims who happened to be Galilean followers of Jesus, the disciples rescued Jesus and shuffled him out of the east gate. They quickly made their way to refuge in Bethany. There Jesus taught.

John Mark found himself fascinated by the logic and humanness of Jesus' philosophy. He listened intently hour after hour as Jesus taught faith, love and rebellion. John Mark clearly believed in the single God and his law. He was a converted Gentile. As the days and nights of tutelage continued, young John Mark became more than fascinated with the philosophy. He became infatuated with Jesus the man.

At the evening communion, Jesus told the myth of the rich man and the beggar.[14] The lesson could have been directed to John Mark.

Jesus began, "Once there was a beggar named Lazarus. He came to the gate of the home of a very rich man. The beggar was covered with sores, his clothes were ragged and dirty. His feet were bloody and disfigured. He felt too weak to prevent the rich man's dog from licking his sores. He begged for crumbs from the rich man's table."

"The rich man stood at the top of the stairs, regal in a purple robe and fine linen. The pitiful beggar was less than human to the pampered ruler. He motioned to his servant to take the beggar away and called the dogs to his side."

"The beggar soon died and was carried by angels to meet our ancestors. Abraham quickly judged him and took him to his bosom as a saint.[15]

"As all humans do, the rich man also died. The ancestors remembered his greed and gluttony. He was assigned to Hell. From that fiery pit of pain and torment, the rich man saw Lazarus beside Abraham. He begged Abraham to allow Lazarus to bring him water so that he could dip his finger into it to cool his burning tongue. Abraham told him that was not possible. The wall between Heaven and Hell could not be crossed after death. Only by obeying the laws of Moses and the prophets during life would one be accepted into the domain of the saints."

"But," added Jesus, "one rose from the dead."

Jesus looked into the eyes of John Mark. "Will you be that rich man?"

"I will give all that I have to the poor and to the cause," responded the young man. "I will be Lazarus. I will live for the cause and die for the cause. My home and my life are yours, Master. I am but a poor beggar."

"Stand, Lazarus," Jesus responded. "You shall die and rise from the dead. I shall instruct you."

The young rich host did not understand Jesus' response. In time, he would.

Another night, Jesus and John Mark walked together to a cabbage garden nearer Jerusalem. The garden belonged to Joseph of Arimathea. It was tended by a resident gardener and its products sold commercially. Large untillable rocks and a low rock cliff filled part of the garden area. In this cliff, Joseph of Arimathea conspired with Jesus to build a tomb.

John Mark, Lazarus, lay upon the ground under a huge rock overhang. Jesus quietly lowered himself on one arm beside him. Jesus admired the soft white skin glistening in the moonlight and gently stroked the young man's forehead. "You are my beloved," Jesus whispered. John Mark's robe fell open.

From that moment on, Jesus referred to John Mark as Beloved Disciple. Many called him Lazarus. One year later, Beloved Disciple waited for the body of Jesus in that same spot beside the tomb.

Jesus sensed that his enemies had begun to realize the extent of his success. He had developed a closely controlled organization of dedicated followers. The seventy select disciples proved very successful in preparing the populace in the countryside to support the Davidians for any showdown with the current governments. The psychological groundwork—winning the hearts and minds of the people—was firm. Of this the enemy was aware but underrated its importance. What the Herodian government and the priestly authorities did not know and could not be allowed to discover was the firm, close-knit cell of Zealot insurgents within the very heart of the government in Jerusalem. It was this cell that Jesus had clandestinely contacted on this trip to the city and over which he had successfully asserted his authority.

The mission was complete in Jerusalem. The danger was increasing. Jesus, Luke, Matthew, Judas Iscariot and Simon Zelotes left Bethany under cover of darkness. They made their way northeastward toward Jericho, avoiding the smooth military rock road for ancient trails across rough terrain.

Jesus and his lieutenants avoided recognition by either the authorities or the Romans while in Jericho. Necessary contacts with fellow insurgents were underground and short-lived. Any public preaching by Jesus would henceforth be limited to more rural areas away from authorities and Roman soldiers and of short duration.

After a rest of three days in Jericho, the group left the city walking directly west. Two days of traversing rough unmarked trails brought them—dirty, tired, hungry and bruised—to the main north-south road that followed the mountain ridge marking the watershed between the River Jordan and the Mediterranean Sea. From the point that intercepted the main road near Bethel and well north of Jerusalem, they began to retrace their recent steps to Capernaum. In the evening shade of Mount Gerizim just outside the city of Sychem, they stopped to recuperate and rest for the evening.

The city of Sychem was a home to an ethnically mixed people collectively known as Samaritans by the Jews. Samaria included several cultural and religious family groups. Long before the time of Jesus, the conquering King Shalmaneser of Assyria placed various people from other defeated regions within the northern half of Israel. Each group had its own God, religion, social mores and cultural identity. The Israelites, who already inhabited the region, understandably felt upset at the forced encroachment. They petitioned the King of Assyria for relief.[16]

The King of Assyria allowed the Israelites to attempt to convert the foreigners in Samaria to the faith of the single God. They met with only limited success. Many Samaritans professed to accept the God of the Jews but they refused to forsake their own gods—Tartak, Adrammelech, Baal and Sepharvaim. They merely added the God of the Jews as one of many. After years of effort, unsuccessful Jewish priests left the unrepentant Samaritans to face divine judgment as non-believers.

The name Samaritan became synonymous to unredeemable sinner. Even Jesus directed his seventy disciples to avoid Samaritans. However, he seemed to disregard his own advice when he personally met Samaritans.

After his lieutenants left the evening campsite to venture into Sychem to buy food and provisions, Jesus walked the short distance from the camp to Jacob's Well. For the Israelite, Jacob's Well held symbolic significance. Here, Jacob, Israel, drew life-sustaining water to nourish the tribe named for his grandson Asher. If Jerusalem was the heart of the Jewish nation, this remote well fed by our earthlocked liquid of life was its soul.[17]

A Samaritan using the well would have been an affront to the hypocritically pious Pharisee, but Jesus appreciated the fact of Humanness before the lie of godliness. Although he well knew that this place was the holy home of his progenitors, Jesus was not upset to see a Samaritan woman drawing water from the well. "May I have a drink of your water?" asked Jesus. "I have no vessel with which to raise it."[18]

"How could you, a Jew, ask me, a Samaritan, for water? Don't you know that Jews are forbidden all contact with Samaritans?" the woman responded.

Jesus answered enigmatically, "If you only knew who asked you for a drink, you would in turn ask him for the gift of living water."

"How could you draw this living water when you have no container? Are you greater than the Jacob of old, who gave us Samaritans the right to use this well while he and his family also drank from it?"

Jesus expanded the puzzle. "Whoever drinks of this well shall become thirsty again, but anyone who drinks the water of which I speak shall live forever."

The curious woman responded, "Sir, give me some of this water, but don't draw it from this well."

"Go, call your husband. Ask him to come here."

"I have no husband."

"Oh, but you do. You have had five husbands, and the man you now live with is not your husband."

Amazed at the psychic power of Jesus, the woman responded, "I perceive that you are a magician. Our fathers worshipped Baal on this mountain. Now you Jews say we should forsake the wisdom of our fathers and worship your single god in Jerusalem. How could I accept your god?"

"There will soon come a time when only Jews will be saved, but you can become a Jew if you accept our beliefs. God is a spirit. They that worship him must worship him in spirit and true believing."

"I have been told that a Jewish Messiah will soon come and he will tell us things similar to what you have said."

Jesus confessed frankly, "I that speak and the Messiah of whom you have heard are one."

At that instant, the disciples returned from the city with provisions. They were shocked to see Jesus talking to a Samaritan Gentile. The woman, also shocked and fearful, dropped her water jar and ran toward the city. There she interrupted the evening confab of some local men. "I have seen him! I have seen the Messiah, the Messiah come to establish a New Kingdom, the Messiah of the Jews."

A quiet old man, the apparent elder of the group, turned to her. "How do you know this Messiah?" he asked, calling her by name. "What sign did he give to you?"

"He knows what is in my mind. He knows all about my past life," she answered.

"We will invite this Jew into the city. We shall see what manner of man he is."

Jesus did go into the city and did speak to the community leaders. He taught them. They came to express belief that a Jesus-led theocracy would benefit them. They would even accept the Jewish God if necessary.

Jesus and his disciples left Samaria ahead of trailing Temple authorities. The priests were even more upset when they learned that Jesus collaborated with Samaritans. The Davidians would appear in one village and the authorities would appear a day or two later. By that time, the Davidians would be gone. Like mosquitoes, the insurgents appeared and disappeared as the authorities tried in vain to pinpoint their activities.

Better received in Galilee and Nazareth than before, Jesus dared not allow a huge audience to congregate to hear him speak. He did heal a few along the road. When he heard that the son of the Mayor of Capernaum was sick, he rushed to that city, staying for a few days before setting off on a fifty mile journey northward.

In council in Peter's house in Capernaum, all agreed that it would be prudent for Jesus to disappear for awhile. Jesus agreed. He and two lieutenants traveled by camel to Caesarea Philippi.[19] A strongly fortified Roman military outpost near the northern limits of Roman control, Caesarea Phillippi prevented incursions from nearby Damascus. There, Jesus and his two disciples rested in the home of the only Essene family in that area while Roman soldiers patrolled the streets outside. A messenger arrived, cutting short their stay. Lazarus was dying.

War

"For in those days shall be affliction, such as was not from the beginning of creation which God created unto this time, neither shall be."

The Holy Bible, Mark 13:19

If Lazarus, John Mark, were to die, the Jerusalem cell and the entire insurgency would suffer a severe blow. John Mark's conversion and rebirth as Lazarus proved invaluable. His love for Jesus guaranteed commitment to death. Not only did Lazarus provide a great deal of material support, he also provided substantial respect as a wise community leader, and as such was irreplaceable. His home in Bethany more resembled a large inn than a private residence.

Indeed, traveling Essenes often tapped his hospitality to provide a retreat, as commanded by Essene law and tradition. Now, Lazarus opened his home to the insurgency as he prepared to give all to a now achievable cause that had been only an Essene dream.

It seemed strange that Jesus did not rush immediately to Lazarus' side. Surely, Jesus could exorcise the demons that possessed the Beloved Disciple. Why then did Jesus tarry two full days in Caesarea Philippi after receiving the summons from Mary and Martha? Because the prearranged day that Jesus should enter the tomb of Lazarus was not yet a camel journey's distance in time![1]

The spiritually reborn John Mark gave more than the poor street beggar whose name he now claimed. He risked his life to test the effects of the drug that included the essential element-that Thomas the Twin had obtained from Simon of Cyrene in Tyre. While this was the same drug that both Jesus' father and his grandfather had used to simulate death, its precise effects had to be known before it would be used to bring about the last days. Jesus needed to confirm exactly how much of the formula would induce a deep, comatose sleep for three days and what medical problems it might induce. Jesus' father Joseph had verbally passed the formula to Jesus but the cause was too important to leave to memory. Lazarus would provide the human verification.

By arriving in Bethany on the day he expected Lazarus to recover from a deep drug-induced coma, Jesus could take full advantage of his supposed death. Jesus tarried almost too long before leaving. On the day he planned to depart, his best camel became lame. That required several hours to negotiate a replacement. With this delay, the van would arrive almost one day later in Bethany than planned. Lazarus would be trapped inside the burial vault much longer than expected. The danger of death from fatigue and thirst was very real. Jesus was understandably worried.

After only two and a half days of travel, Jesus and his caravan approached Bethany. The camels sensed that the long trip was nearing an end.

The home of Lazarus, Mary and Martha dominated the first sight of the village. Most large homes were located to the near west side of Jerusalem, directly opposite the Bethany homestead. Bethany made a more convenient location for Essene priests who sometimes traveled from Qumran to visit the Temple. Operational plans for the coming insurrection conferred a prominent role. Within its walls, two dozen officers could sleep in the accommodations. A well-stocked storehouse had been prepared, along with the large cache of weapons now hidden beneath its floor. Without Lazarus, all plans would need revising.

As Jesus and his lieutenants entered Bethany, all was quiet. The few who walked the streets did so in silence, heads hung low and eyes focused two steps ahead. No one met the travelers at the outer gate of the Lazarus home. They entered the front courtyard and in respect began to bathe in preparation to enter the main house. The two sisters, Mary and Martha, entered the courtyard from the main house, clearly consumed in grief. Seeing Jesus, both ran to him with tears streaming down their faces. "He is dead," they cried. "They have killed him. He is in the tomb, never again to grace our home."[2]

Jesus appeared visibly shaken when he heard of Lazarus' death. He wept openly. The death of Lazarus would be very troubling to the Messiah on two counts: not only would he have lost a dear friend and lover, but he also well knew that it could inflict a serious blow to the insurgency. Lazarus' popularity with the people allowed him to support the cause with some immunity. Caiaphas, the High Priest of Judea, and Herod Archelaus refrained from arresting Lazarus for fear of a general and spontaneous revolt of the people. They were elated to learn of his supposed death.

Lazarus was found dying alongside the Jerusalem-Jericho highway three miles east of his home. He lay in the middle of a well-traveled section of the road. Some questions were never answered. There were no marks on his body or any other clue as to the cause of death. He had told Mary and Martha that he intended to meet some important Sadducees at the edge of the city. Why had he traveled so far along the highway toward Jericho on foot without his man-servant? Who were the Sadducees whom he was to meet? How did Lazarus die? Many people of Bethany sensed the answers. None dared utter their thoughts aloud.

Jesus knew, as well as any, that the Sadducees Lazarus met four days earlier were Temple police. When the Sanhedrin secretly decided that Lazarus must be killed, one member offered a plan that would leave no clues. The Temple police gave Lazarus a poison drink that had been provided to them by a prominent member of the Sanhedrin, Joseph of Arimathea. Lazarus knew he would pass into a coma. Before he lost consciousness, he positioned himself where he was sure to be discovered.

Jesus seemed to repress his grief quickly. He was now key to a successful completion of the scheme.

Jesus realized the insurgency would benefit from the incident if the people believed Lazarus somehow overcame the power of the government and still lived. The personal popularity of Lazarus could not be allowed to die. To keep him alive in the minds of the people would be a formidable task for Jesus if he actually died.

There was a foreboding sense of danger in and around the house of Lazarus. It was filled with people of all castes and vocations. Jewish bureaucrats from nearby Jerusalem mixed freely with the mourners. Many were known to be Sadducees. Some even sat inside the living area of the house. It was obvious the High Priest had dispatched his intimates to gather whatever intelligence possible on the insurgency and its supporters.

Into this tense atmosphere walked the theocratic leader of the movement. An aura of subtle power surrounded him. His clean, radiant purple robe identified him as King. Now it was the Temple spies who trembled in fear. They tried to hide their fear with forced mockery. "Behold, how he loved him!", they laughed. Jesus did not return the ridicule.

"Your brother shall rise again," Jesus said to Martha and Mary. "Take me to the vault where he sleeps."

Jesus, Mary, and Martha walked alone to the cliff-side tomb. The Temple spies did not follow. Their bravery disappeared at the prospect of seeing the dead Lazarus.

It is said the three mourners removed the huge stone that entombed Lazarus. Although Mary and Martha protested that the four-day old dead body would stink, Jesus approached Lazarus and cried out for him to awaken.

Rumor soon spread throughout the community that Lazarus was alive. Before long many eye witnesses vied to tell the most intriguing story about seeing Lazarus alive and healthy. Those rumors rippled out into Jerusalem and the Judean countryside. The reputation of Jesus was such that the rumors would have soon become truth even if the drug had killed Lazarus. In fact, the drug and the plan worked perfectly, producing a major coup for the insurgency.

Jewish authorities reacted in fear. They removed the stone from the tomb of Lazarus.Only his linen graveclothes remained. Lazarus was alive!

In Jerusalem, Caiaphas called a council of his chief priests. The problem to be discussed was the popularity of Jesus to which they attributed his many miracles. The priests were very aware that they ruled at the pleasure of Herod Archelaus who, in turn, derived his power from the Roman occupation force. If Jesus' New Kingdom -- a challenge to all authority --were to gain the support of an overwhelming mass of the people, their positions of power would be in serious jeopardy.

Caiaphas addressed his chief priests: "......it is expedient for us that one man should die for the people so that the whole nation shall not perish. If we let him (Jesus) alone, all men will believe on him, and the Romans shall come and take away our positions and our nation."[3]

It was thus decided that Jesus must be put to death. But Jesus, and his disciples, had now disappeared.

The small band of insurgents reappeared in an Essene home in a small town called Ephraim.[4] From there Jesus sent word to the other officers to immediately depart Capernaum for Ephraim. The fifteen were soon in council.[5] A new strategy in response to the Caiaphas threat was necessary.

Jesus dominated the meeting. He left no doubt that he was the Master. The Zealot organization had pledged allegiance to the House of David and to Jesus. It was now important to define the lines of command/control and ensure understanding of and compliance to the principles of insurgent warfare in a theocratic setting.

Jesus commissioned twelve of the inner circle to go singularly into the countryside, find each of the seventy disciples and instigate controlled terror against the Romans, the priestly authorities, and all loyal to the Herods.

"You shall heal," Jesus decreed. "I command you to heal and to tell all who will listen that the end is near."

"Do we attempt to convert Pharisees to your teaching? Do we debate?"

"Beware. Beware of the power of the doctrine that is taught by the Pharisees and the Sadducees. That which comes from the mouth of a pious Pharisee is trash. You must not allow this trash to soil the logic of the true word. Do not allow Pharisees into your confidence. They are like sleeping dogs in a cattle manger - they will not eat nor will they allow the cattle to eat. The Pharisees and the scribes have taken the keys of knowledge and hidden them. They do not enter the vault of knowledge nor do they allow those who would follow them to do so. When among Pharisees you must be as shrewd as snakes and as innocent as doves. Without a cognitive philosophy we could not hope to gain the support of the populace."

Jesus continued, reminding the disciples of the horror of the undertaking at hand,[6]"I tell you, the war that is upon us will be more horrible than you can imagine. You have read the terrible predictions of wars described by ancient prophets such as Zachariah and Isaiah. As you know, all those prophecies have been fulfilled. The Jewish nation has suffered much. But all the suffering of the past that was induced by foreign enemies shall be as a finger prick compared to that which will erupt from the pungent forces within the very soul of our land. Since God created all things, there has been no time as sorrowful and afflicting as we shall endure. The great buildings that we know shall be destroyed; not one stone shall be left upon another. Babies shall die because their mother's breasts give poison milk. Brother shall betray brother, and children shall rise up against their parents. Israel shall be destroyed so that you may rebuild it for the Kingdom's sake."

"You must be alert. Do not be drunk when the time comes. Many of you will die. Others will be brought before councils and sentenced to death. You must die in silence. Those who do not betray their comrades will be rewarded with everlasting life. If any would betray the cause he will die a thousand deaths.

This is the holiest of holy wars. You must follow your orders without question and trust God. I will rise up to the Kingship when we have won."

Jesus spoke of the lawful succession to the Davidian Kingship. "I have been asked who will become King if I die. I now tell you that it must be James,[7] the son of Mary and Zebedee. For his sake, heaven and earth were revealed to me as he loved me as an older brother since I was a baby in my mother's womb."

As he neared the end of his command lecture to his lieutenants, Jesus emphasized the most important principle of insurgent warfare - comradeship. "As he who commands me[8] has done so in love, so I command you in love. You must love one another as I have loved you. You must give your life before you reveal any secrets of the insurgency. You are not servants. You are fighters for the New Kingdom. Your great love for the cause cannot be better demonstrated than that you lay down your life for your comrades. No less is expected of you. No more can be given. You will be free to testify, tell all, after the New Kingdom is established."

"Now go, my comrades. Contact the seventy. Tell them the time is now. We begin. You will find me in contemplation in Capernaum. There I will instruct you further."

Insurgent war spread throughout the land. The exact source of the insurgency eluded government counter-efforts: every layer of insurgent activity was insulated from all others by a code of honor which required secrecy until death.

Each of the seventy developed local covert organizations. As each disciple was separated from the superior by fear of everlasting torment, so too each operative within each organization could not be linked to any higher command. When captured, warriors would only profess loyalty to the single God even when submitted to the most cruel torture.

Most terrorist targets were carefully selected by the insurgents for effect upon the populace. The object of insurgent operations was to win the support of the people. Random violence was strictly avoided unless it could be blamed on the Roman occupiers or their Herodian dupes. When a local government official was killed the people knew him as an enemy and saw a government that was unable to protect its own. Camels were killed, water supplies poisoned, roads obstructed, fields burned and sheep stolen, but the only victims were those who supported the governments. Not infrequently seen was the most prized possession of the local priest, his imported carpet, burning in a most public place. Whatever helped win the hearts and minds of the people was within limits.

Persuasive tactics were not all negative terrorism. The disciples of the inner circle and the seventy performed miracles in the name of Jesus. They healed those who believed or might come to believe in the cause. Food stolen from the enemy was distributed to possible recruits. A reverse system of tribute saw money taken from the authorities and given to the poor. Disciples often physically helped those in need by performing such tasks as repairing homes or tilling a garden. These activities made the insurgents appear as altruistic champions of the poor.

Jesus said, "Those who are not against us are for us." Thus any insurgent who would steal from or force themselves on any undecided person was sanctioned. This was in sharp contrast to the arrogant and roughshod acquisition methods often perpetrated by Roman soldiers and Temple police.

Some terrorism was directed at lower ranking Roman soldiers and Temple policemen. The constant fear of the assassin or, worse, the kidnapper, affected military performance and adversely influenced morale. The favorite weapon of the assassin was the *sicarii*.[9] This was a small sickle-shaped sword keenly sharpened on the inside of the half-moon cradle. An unwary soldier or policeman would feel his head suddenly pulled back just as the sicarii cut through his wind-pipe. The helpless victim could not utter a sound as he fell dead to the ground. This act of terror happened in crowded markets as well as in dark alleys: who in a crowd would dare identify an insurgent and bring sure death to himself? Soldiers and police never knew where death might lurk. Since they could not identify the enemy, they came to feel the entire population was against them. This feeling led to many unwarranted acts of repression against the people that helped insurgent efforts to recruit undecided persons to their side.

The kidnapped often fared worse than the murdered. If he were lucky, a kidnapped authority would be held for prisoner trade. More likely, he would suffer a horrible and slow death and have his mutilated body displayed in a public place as warning to all those who would not support the Kingdom of God.

By command of God, as relayed to them by Jesus Messiah, the insurgents wrote nothing of the terroristic campaign. They did not talk of their personal success or failure as physicians and exorcists: to do so might reflect upon the great magician himself. Later, it was recorded that the disciples were individually preaching and recruiting in the field during the last year of Jesus' life.

Despite faithful obedience to the command of silence and secrecy, hundreds of Israelites were convicted of crimes against the State and condemned to death by Roman courts. Because the guilty would not confess, many innocent were also executed.

Roman military courts became solely responsible for punishment in matters of sedition: authority to punish rebels was assumed by Pontius Pilate when he felt the Jewish Sanhedrin abused that power to its own ends. Crucifixion was the prescribed punishment for insurgency. The countryside was spotted with crosses in the year thirty-six.

Not directly linked to the Davidian/Zealot activities was an undisciplined riot in Jerusalem.[10] Passions of the people exploded when an augmented Roman military detachment diverted some water from an aqueduct leading to the Essene quarter for their own needs. A leader in the person of Barabbas emerged to urge the crowd to rush Fort Antonia. Some bloodshed ensued before the rioters were beaten back and Barabbas captured. Pontius Pilate detained Barabbas for a possible prisoner swap, but his efforts were frustrated when the mainline insurgents showed little interest in Barabbas' welfare.

The twelve of the inner circle returned, one by one, to the home of Simon Peter in Capernaum. Jesus and Beloved Disciple awaited them. Each of the twelve reported that the seventy were highly successful. The psychological ground was well tilled. The populace tensely awaited the long expected Messiah, King of Israel, Son of David. The authorities and the Romans were in disarray. Their every attempt to pacify the people seemed only to build more distrust. If they promised to build new public facilities such as roads or water wells, the people believed it was only in response to insurgent activities: if they didn't they were deemed repressive. If they captured and punished suspected terrorists, they were murderers of the children of Israel: if they didn't they were helpless bunglers. The groundwork was completed for the climatic event, but certain precise conditions had to be met before the end.

Jesus was a great manipulator of the superstitious nature of the children of the Kingdom of David. He knew and understood the demons and devils that were so real in their daily lives. He often demonstrated that he could overcome those evil forces by changing the mind-set of the afflicted. Nothing in the scriptures handed down by ancient prophets required the coming messiah to exorcise and heal, it was simply an expected quality of any wise teacher in those days.

The scriptures did expect the promised Messiah to perform miracles. The populace told many stories of the magical powers of Jesus such as his speaking from the cradle, walking on water, and raising Lazarus from the dead. If these magical feats were not credible, it mattered little. The more the stories were circulated the closer to irrefutable truths they became. The farther in distance and longer in time it became from the actual incident, the greater was any given miracle.

The philosophy of Jesus was the third leg upon which a constituency was built. This philosophy was responsive to peasant concerns. It de-emphasized commercialism and relaxed social rules that were based upon priestly infallibility. In effect, it was an attack upon both the power of the Temple and the Roman Empire. In his parables and words of wisdom, Jesus suggested a simpler, less structured life that might exist under his rule.

Cause is the essential ingredient of war. Cause -- defending the status quo, bringing God to the heathens, building socialism, defending the faith. Economics always underlies cause, but can never be admitted to be the cause: not by the leadership of your side, anyway. Antagonists must have cause or there can be no war.

The insurgent war in which Jesus became both the principle leader and the godhead was, like all wars, based upon economics, but cloaked in the right and good. The descendants of David felt they should enjoy elevated positions in society. This included not only the satisfaction and utility of status, but also greatly enhanced economic opportunity. The Roman and Herodian government locked the Davidians out of what they considered their right. The war was between the elite and the would-be elite. The populace, that huge mass of lower human-ity, were only pawns on the chessboard, but both sides knew that whoever won the pawns must win the game.

In Capernaum, Jesus was very pleased with the reports of his lieutenants. He felt the stage was ready for the final phase of insurgency -- open rebellion and overt warfare. He had established himself as the Messiah promised by ancients as well as contemporary preachers. Now he must make certain that a precise chain of events came about. The people had been told many times how the new King would ascend to power. The ascendancy of Jesus would have to fit those preconceived notions.

Jesus said, "The time is now. We must return to Jerusalem to begin the last days."

War Fellowship

"Verily I say unto you, all these things shall come upon this generation."

The Holy Bible, Matthew 23:36

The entire inner circle prepared for a final journey to Jerusalem. The caravan was fairly large and would have been conspicuous to government authorities had it not been near the time of Passover—the season of thousands of pilgrimages into Jerusalem.

Still, the fifteen principals on camels and several personal servants leading pack animals were in some danger of detection, but Jesus felt the likely favorable impact of openness upon the populace outweighed the dangers. He was certain the people were ready for open rebellion. It was clear to any who cared to look, Jesus led the caravan as King of all Israel. He magnificently sat high atop the finest of animals, the harness and gear adorned with fine jewels of the East. His brilliant purple robe shone in the bright sunlight, revealing a unique tailoring feature—there were no seams in the sleeved garment that slid over the head and arms as would an armor coat molded out of a single piece of copper.[1] He was King to all who looked upon him.

Some would do no more than steal a glance at Jesus and the van. These were lower level government scribes and bureaucrats. If they saw and did not report, they could face severe punishment from the government. If they saw and did attempt to summon police, they would face eventual death at the hands of terrorists, if not the general population.

The openness of Jesus led many to excited anticipation. The end was now. The beginning began. There seemed to be little that the Romans and priestly authorities dared do to stop the sure procession of the new king to the Temple with obvious intent to ascend to the true Kingship. The word spread like frightened doves. Surely, the Kingdom of David would return as promised on this Passover. Surely, this was the Messiah whom God anointed King.

Although this was not a recruiting trip, Jesus did not deny those who came to him to be healed. In the small village of Ephraim in Samaria, the van stopped to rest within friendly and familiar surroundings. As they and the camels washed and drank the water of the town well, ten lepers watched from a distance. The lepers cried, "Jesus, Master, have mercy on us."[2]

Jesus walked over to the lepers and said to them, "Go. Show yourselves to the priests. Tell them who sent you." The ten walked toward the local temple. As they walked the leper sores disappeared and they were cured. The priests personally knew each leper. When the lepers entered the temple with no signs of leprosy the priests were terrified. They had heard of Jesus and been ordered to detain him. Instead, they ran to the caves of the nearby hills.

Only one leper returned to the village center to give thanks to Jesus. That leper was the only Samaritan of the otherwise Jewish group of ten.[3]

In another town, a rich young ruler secretly approached the camp of Jesus and his lieutenants. He asked Jesus, "Good Master, what must I do to receive eternal life?"[4]

Jesus responded tartly, "Why do you call me good. Only God is good. I am not God. I only strive to do good. But, if you would have life, real life, you must obey the Ten Commandants of Moses."

"That I have done since youth, yet I do not feel fulfilled."

"Then I say to you, you must sell all you own, give the receipts to the poor, leave your family and your easy way of life, and follow the cause."

The young man was not willing to do as Jesus commanded. He could not give up the family life and luxury he so treasured. He turned and sorrowfully walked away, never to experience the fullness of inner contentment.

Jesus was visibly angry at the rejection. He turned to his disciples and pointed to a camel. "I say to you, it is easier for a camel to pass through the eye of a needle than it is for a rich man to be part of the Kingdom of God."[5]

Jesus went on to promise each disciple dominion over one of the twelve tribes and again declared that only those persons who were willing to forsake their entire family and all earthly possessions for the cause would be welcome in the New Kingdom. As he had promised before, he said those who totally dedicated themselves to the cause would receive everlasting life, but this time suggested that this perpetual life would be in heaven, not on earth. He previously taught that heaven was reserved for those who came from there. In either case, it was clear that those who gave their lives for the Holy War would live.

The next morning during the breaking of the night's fast, Jesus attempted to explain how those who fought for the cause would be awarded. To the chagrin of those who had come to Jesus and the Davidians as long-time Zealot fighters, Jesus said that in the New Kingdom those recent converts to the cause might receive more than veterans. "Many that were first shall be last, and last may be first."[6] This rubbed Peter Zelote: he had expected to be most rewarded because of his early Zealot connection, but he did realize that Jesus had been acting and speaking rather strangely lately. Perhaps it was due to anxiety over the near future. Surely, Jesus would regain a more consistent approach to practical matters after the end. The caravan broke camp and departed from the small village on the last leg into Jerusalem. The Mountain of Olives came into sight as the travelers intercepted the Jericho/Jerusalem military road a few miles west and below Bethany. The mountain hid the final destination from view but Bethany, the evening's objective, soon became discernible.

The road was jammed with pilgrims destined for Passover in the Holy City. Jesus walked among the crowd: a servant led his mount some distance behind. In spite of his attempt to mingle unnoticed in the crowd, many recognized Jesus as the King/Messiah. Jesus brushed them aside with such words as "Soon. Soon. Very soon, it shall be! You must be silent and wait patiently. Do not hint to anyone until tomorrow morning. Then, you may welcome with shouts of joy and great enthusiasm the triumphant entry of the King of all Israel. Please, wait and tell no one until time is right."[7]

In Bethany, Jesus and his fourteen intimates walked directly toward the home of Lazarus. The servants reigned the animals to the water troughs near the city water well. There the animals would drink their fill and the servants would bathe. The officers would cleanse themselves in the luxurious garden baths of the Lazarus home in preparation for a communal meal.

The short distance from the well to the house was blocked by a crowd of enthusiastic followers and some who hoped for a healing miracle from Jesus. Jesus had no time for the multitude on this important evening. Nightfall was fast approaching and he had much to tell his lieutenants. Peter brandished a short two-edged military sword and the crowd opened to allow the fifteen to push their way through. After the group was securely inside the entrance garden, the outside gate was closed and bolted to block the excited people. A disciple reported to Jesus that his mother, Holy Mary, was outside. Jesus instructed the disciples to dismiss her, explaining "I must be about my father's business."

Simon the Leper had maintained the house while Lazarus was with Jesus. He welcomed the weary warriors. It was clear that he no longer coveted the title Prince of Israel. He embraced Jesus and clearly pronounced him King of Israel. Jesus accepted the commission without comment.

As the inner circle bathed, Mary and Martha walked through the main door and entered the garden. They dropped their white robes and stepped into the pool. It was required that they too ceremoniously cleanse themselves because they would partake of communion with the rest.

Jesus sat on the edge of the pool, his feet dangled in the still water. Beloved Disciple sat on one side of him and Mary Magdalene on the other. Mary of Bethany approached Jesus. She knelt in the shallow water, placed the feet of Jesus in the vortex formed by her closed legs and lower body, and poured expensive imported oil upon the feet of an obviously pleased Messiah from a small, finely-crafted ewer. "You must accept this anointing as you are most worthy," she said. "I anoint you, Jesus, King of Israel and Savior of the Jewish nation. Long may you live." She then wiped the excess oil from Jesus' feet with her long, black hair and tossed her head to propel the hair behind her body away from her face.

None dared to question the anointing. All accepted Jesus as the King of the Jews, but one piously scrutinized the cost. Judas, as treasurer of the insurgent organization, protested the luxury. "Jesus, why do you accept this extravagance? Do you not teach that we, as molders of the minds of the populace, must live the lifestyle of the poor? You have instructed us to give up all our personal possessions and daily depend upon God for food and shelter. Could not this oil be sold and the proceeds given to the poor?"

Jesus felt compassion for Mary. She had performed an act of love, honor, and respect, only to be berated by Judas. Jesus spoke more in her behalf than in his own defense. At first, his words seemed strangely uncharacteristic as he tried to explain that costs were of little importance in this, perhaps the most important anointment in history. "The poor shall always be with us. I must soon leave. Let this woman show her love by this small act. The money that could be gained from the sale of this oil would little help the poor, but the comfort this woman receives from this act of love will long sustain her."

Judas understood. He bowed his head in thoughtful silence. The near future presented only anxious uncertainty.

Simon the Leper had supervised the preparation of the meal and seemed to act as master of the household. John Mark, 'Lazarus,' acted as the guest that he was after an absence of almost one year. Simon beckoned Jesus and Lazarus to recline at the head of the long dining mat. The disciples scrambled for position.

Jesus began the fellowship dinner. He held his freshly filled wineglass high in salute. "This is the blood of life," he recited, "drink, for it must sustain us into the New Kingdom." He took a loaf of bread from a large basket and tore a piece for himself. He passed one half to Beloved Disciple on his right. "Eat," he commanded. "Eat, for bread is the staff of life."

Slaves from Cyrene carried tray after tray of fruits and meats from the cooking area. In addition to traditional lamb and fish, Simon presented a special dish, chicken, recently introduced to the region, roasted in olive oil, butter, and garlic. An uneaten roasted whole dove, symbolic of the poor, remained on the dining rug as if a centerpiece. Sweet chestnuts, dates, figs, grapes, cheese and honey completed the offering. Red wine flowed freely.

Simon the Leper darted from couch to couch, excited by his host duties on this important occasion. Mary sat at the end of the mat. Martha helped serve.

Almost two hours passed in resolute gluttony after Jesus' pre-dinner remarks. Little was spoken. Some of the disciples leaned back onto posh pillows and dozed. Finally, Jesus rose and all were alert and attentive.

Jesus began to speak with rallying words. "These are the last days before the establishment of the New Kingdom. For those against us it is the end. We must use every care. Each must perform his duties with precision and determination. Any slip could doom our entire enterprise to failure. We have many fighters with us located throughout the land of David: some are not trained and ready for disciplined combat, but I trust the seventy to lead them with skill. There are three hundred invaluable guerrillas within the walls of Jerusalem: some are in the highest councils of government. We have no heavy war equipment, nor should we need it. Our greatest asset, my Sons of God, is the people. They love us and respect our cause. We shall win, but first I must die."[9]

"Within two days we can expect the return of an augmented Roman cohort from Caesarea with fresh orders. They are well trained and equipped, but their heavy weapons and horse-driven chariots are of little value within the city walls. They are not ready to fight a war that starts from the heart and spreads outward."

"We also must deal with five thousand ruling priests and the Temple police, however, the priests are helpless without the support of the people. The people are on our side. We shall win, but first I must die."[8]

He then issued specific instructions: "Two disciples will steal into the night. You will find a pure white donkey. I will ride that donkey on our triumphant entry into the Temple tomorrow. I command you to take the donkey by whatever means necessary." Jesus well knew that the donkey would be staked out by secret operatives. [9]

Later, in the early morning hours, the two disciples found a beautiful white donkey colt hobbled for the night. The donkey was part of a Passover pilgrimage caravan camped at the fork of the road from Bethany to the eastern gates of the Temple. The small valley of Kidron, just east of the Temple, restricted easy access to the eastern gates. Faithful pilgrims camped there very near the gates intending to enter Jerusalem at first light of day.

As the disciples were untying the donkey it brayed and woke the camp. The pilgrims were surprised to see two armed men stealing such an important property. "Lo," one disciple blurted out, "This donkey is destined for glory! And you who give it to the cause of God shall enjoy everlasting peace. Tomorrow the Messiah who is King shall enter the Temple on the back of this very animal. You should make ready the Savior's entry by lining the path with palm tree leaves and garments."

The pilgrims seemed more impressed with the disciple's weapons than by their words. However, they had heard rumors of the approach of an insurgent army led by the 'Great Teacher.' They agreed to prepare the path to the Temple as suggested and timidly allowed the strangers to lead the young donkey away. By the time Jesus mounted the donkey for his final ride that afternoon, the operatives within the camp had worked the crowd into a frenzy of anticipation.

At the fellowship dinner, Jesus had more orders to issue. He turned to Simon Peter and John Boanerges. "We shall have our Passover fellowship meal at the home of the father of my beloved. Because it would be too dangerous for my beloved to enter the city at this time, I command you to go and find the home which is within the Essene quarter. You will notice the entrance is guarded by a sculpture that appears to be a male human carrying a water vase on his head as if he were a woman. Approach that entrance and identify yourself as liaison officers of the Master. Check the chambers for security and be sure the dining hall is sufficient. You will note the hall's position is well above street level. This should make it easy to defend if that becomes necessary. Brief well the guerrilla guards as to the number and make-up of our staff. There should be no problem. I have deep trust in the ability and loyalty of our underground within the city walls."[10]

Jesus motioned Mary of Bethany to approach his position. He took her hands in his and spoke as would a father counseling his child. "I will tell you well," he began. "You must know the secret of my father and grandfather. Hear it once, and never tell another."

"Before I was born, the elder Annas accused my earthly father, Joseph, of secretly marrying my mother, Mary. Annas claimed my conception was natural, of the man Joseph. The priest judges considered the charges in lawful court. They ruled that Joseph would test the will of God by drinking a poison passed down by the ancients. But in order to insure the prophecies were fulfilled and the insurrection they themselves planned secure, they slightly changed the formula of the drink. A normal, healthy man who drank the new compound would not die but would pass into a deep coma that resembles death. Within three days the effect of the drink would pass and the man awaken. Among my few personal possessions, there by the wall, is a bottle of that liquid. It is based upon mandrake, wine vinegar, and precious *silphium laciniatum* from Cyrene.[11] You must hold that bottle secure in your safekeeping. Bring it to Jerusalem the day after two nights. At the right time, you will know when, I will ask you for a drink from it. When I pass into a coma you must weep and wail. An operative will be allowed to quickly remove my body to the tomb we have discussed. Do as I command. The success of the cause and my life depends upon you."

Only Lazarus seemed to understand. He knew well the drug of which Jesus spoke. He was pleased that his role had proved so important to his lover's plans.

Jesus turned to his consort and said, "You, Beloved Disciple, have a critical role. You will carry water, healing ointments, and food to the tomb. Hide. Wait there until my body is placed in that cold place. I will eagerly anticipate your loving hands anointing my body when I awake."

He next addressed Simon Peter. "Peter, you will remain, as always, near me. Your protection and vigilance is more important than ever at this critical time. I am comforted by your presence. You know that! But now you must be prepared to deny me. You must live so the cause will live. Do not interfere with my arrest or trial. I shall return. Retire to the background and deny you know me or anything about the insurrection. I shall see you in the glory of the New Kingdom.[12]

"Judas, my faithful treasurer, yours is the most difficult task of all. You must insure that I am arrested and brought before the authorities. Find Annas and Caiaphas. Convince them to take you to Herod. Herod knows, but is afraid to openly acknowledge, that I am the true theocratic leader of the Kingdom of David. Tell him that we intend to overthrow his surrogate potentate, run his Roman masters out, and create a Godly empire based upon the law of the Torah. Tell him you have had a change of heart and are ready to help him round up the conspirators, beginning with me. Do this tomorrow night just prior to midnight and the beginning of the third day of Passover. Do not despair. It is as it must be. Betray me, but give your life before you betray any other comrade."[13]

"God is our power. King David is our inspiration. The song that David wrote so many years ago shall be repeated all over the land of David this Passover. The people have preconceived convictions that a certain precise set of events must precede the New Kingdom. The most deeply rooted belief is that the Messiah who shall be King must die and, like Lazarus, raise from the dead. We shall make certain that the prophesies of David and the ancients are fulfilled as the populace would have them. We begin with the triumphant entry tomorrow."

"Gentlemen," Jesus swept his outstretched right arm across the room to demonstrate he was addressing each person, "do not needlessly risk your lives. The cause needs each one of you alive. Nothing can stop our momentum. The Kingdom of God is imminent. The people shall rise up in revolt against the evil priests who now serve Rome, not God. Be in the midst of the masses when revolt explodes. Guide them to our cause. You shall inherit the Kingdom of David."

Jesus cautioned his lieutenants to maintain security. "Never, never tell man what I have instructed here tonight. Tomorrow evening we will dine again in fellowship. That council will be completely for public consumption: there is a spy in the household staff and I intend to use him for our purposes. I expect the enemy to hear and report the proceedings of tomorrow's fellowship, precisely. Remember, tonight's orders override anything you might hear from me within the city walls. Here, in the spiritual presence of my dear friends, everything is in confidence."

These were the last orders Jesus would give. He emptied his wine glass and reclined on his dining couch. Some of the disciples slipped away as Jesus continued to think aloud with little care of his audience.

Dawn broke.

Jerusalem was deceptively quiet. Despite one hundred thousand pilgrims camped around the city walls, the only sounds were that of animals greeting the new day's light. The tragedies of recent days weighed heavily upon the mood of the people. Civil riots had left eighteen dead at the tower of Siloam and many, including the young man named Barabbas, were jailed for sedition.[14]

The quiet was not gloom—the people seemed to expect the appearance of the Davidian King/Messiah this very Holy Week.

Pontius Pilate, the Roman governor-general of all Palestine, made a seemingly small and inadvertent mistake. The civil disturbances had proved worrisome and tiring to the cohort of about six hundred troops positioned at Fort Antonia. Pilate was temporarily in residence with his wife at the fort. From there, he released part of the weary cohort before replacements arrived from his normal headquarters in Caesarea That order proved to come at a most inopportune time to be under-strength.

Jesus and his immediate staff walked from Bethany toward Jerusalem. The Messiah halted his small entourage near a rock mound within sight of the Temple gates of Jerusalem. There he climbed upon a large boulder and delivered his last sermon.[15]

Thousands of pilgrims, most of them picked for loyalty by local operatives, listened. Within the multitude were nine hundred armed insurgents awaiting the victory march into the Temple.

"The scribes and the authorities sat in the seat of power that was established by Moses. They wrap themselves in the trappings of office and ask to be called Teacher. For you there is only one teacher, I, Messiah and your master. The evil ones insist upon long, pretentious public prayer. I say to you, they shall be punished for such hypocrisy in my Kingdom."

Jesus looked to the sky and shouted, "Woe to you, scribes and authorities. You appear clean and bright on the outside, but are filled with filth and death on the inside. Woe to you, blind leaders. Woe to you who love the gold of the Temple, but know not the word. Woe to you, the children of those who killed prophets. Today you die. Today the righteous blood of Abel and all his descendants until Zechariah shall bring vengeance upon you. Today you die."

The crowd worked into a frenzy. Those nearest Jesus, mostly women and children, threw their arms into the air shouting, "Save us, save us, Son of David. Glory to the King! Glory to the King! Long reign over us!"

Behind the women and children, farther from Jesus, a large contingent of more militant men seemed to respond on a pre-set cue: "Lord, Lord, King of all Israel, lead us to the Temple."

Swords flashed. Spears protruded above the crowd. Occasionally a leather shield could be noticed. It was clear that if the Temple police were to attempt to repress their own people, the costs would be dear.

The white donkey colt that the two disciples had purloined was led through the throng of people. Jesus' demeanor changed. Suddenly he appeared as the peaceful righteous teacher. His head bowed in apparent thought and contemplation. He touched the donkey gently and slipped onto its back.

Miraculously, the young, never ridden colt accepted the load without protest. Had the occasion not been so towering, the sight might have been comical: a fat, red-faced little man, both legs dangling from one side of the tiny animal, perched gingerly on the slippery back, beginning a historic ride of triumph and doom.

The ride of victory began. Jesus, balanced upon the small white donkey, did not smile or seem to acknowledge the crowd. He occasionally glanced up toward the Temple gate from an otherwise expressionless, empty gaze. The gate remained open. Not a single policeman was to be seen. The reduced Roman garrison seemed not to move within Fort Antonia. This moment belonged to the Davidians—there could be no question but that Jesus was King.

Thousands of people lined the road to the east gate. Deafening cheers of joy and hope followed the new King up the road as he and the donkey slowly progressed toward the Temple. Palm leaves, by custom reserved for returning conquerors, carpeted the path. In frenzied excitement, some followers threw their clothes on the dusty ground as a sign of complete troth to Jesus. All shouted praise and encouragement. Gone were pleas for salvation; instead only expressions of victory won thundered to the new King. "Praise, King of Israel. Begin. Begin. Begin. Long live the King. Death to the traitors of our ancestors."[16]

Into the courtyard of the Temple marched Jesus flanked by armed zealots. The very people that Jesus had previously condemned, merchants of blasphemous trinkets, money lenders, and peddlers of pleasures, lined the courtyard. As they became aware that the noise and commotion announced the arrival of Jesus, the budding capitalists scurried for cover. Many were chased down and captured by the insurgents. Without trials nor heed for their cries for mercy, the conquerors tied the merchants to make-shift whipping posts. Jesus physically beat and verbally scourged as many as he could before exhaustion overcame him. He and his lieutenants quietly retired to the upper room of the house of Beloved Disciple's father.[17]

Jesus slept.

As sundown approached, the Roman military detachment from Caesarea marched past the Palace of Herod and entered the Gennath Gate. Suddenly, all was quiet. No person could be found who had seen the King. No weapons were seen.

Everyone seemed to have business somewhere else as they quickly moved along the streets. Even the Temple merchants, so recently terrorized, could remember nothing. High Priest Caiaphas and Governor/General Pilate conferred. They agree that tomorrow, with the aid and council of Herod, they would sweep the city for the insurgents. Jesus would surely be caught and suffer death for sedition.

They knew it was the last supper together. Without proper ceremonial cleansing of their bodies they lay at the mats that had been prepared as a grand celebration of victory. Roman soldiers scoured the streets directly below their third story refuge.

The leaders of the recent moment of victory trusted renewed triumph would come quickly, within three days. They looked to the man who sat in a lotus position at the end of the serving mat for words of hope and assurance.

Jesus' eyes were closed, his head bowed toward his open knees, his arms dangled limply to the floor. He seemed in a trance. When he did begin to speak, the words were not his. He chanted ancient and familiar songs of the great King David and his musicians. Haunting, melodic words of war, pain, love, and praise of God filled the large room. He sang of God's promise to David and his descendants.[18]

> "I will sing of the mercies of the Lord forever:
> with my mouth will I make known thy
> faithfulness to all generations.
>
> For I have said, Mercy shall be built up forever:
> thy faithfulness shalt thou establish in the very heavens.
>
> I have made a covenant with my chosen,
> I have sworn unto David my servant,
> Thy seed will I establish forever,
> and build up thy throne to all generations."

As Jesus finished the ancient song it was clear he was the anointed one. He said not another word. He remained absolutely still, trance-like. Peter began another song. Soon the entire assemblage chanted the well-known words.[19]

> "Give the King thy judgments, O God,
> and thy righteousness unto the King's son.

He shall judge thy people with righteousness,
and the poor with judgment.

The mountains shall bring peace to the people,
and the little hills, by righteousness.

He shall judge the poor of the people,
he shall save the children of the needy,
and shall break in pieces the oppressor.

They shall fear thee as long as the sun and moon endure,
throughout all generations......

He shall have dominion also from sea to sea,
and from river unto the ends of the
earth.........
And he shall live,
and to him shall be given the gold of Sheba:......

.........and men shall be blessed in him:
and all nations shall call him blessed........."

The song of praise to the new King/Messiah complete, He
answered with a denunciation of the wicked priests and unclean
Romans.[20]

"Do ye indeed speak righteousness, O congregation?
Do ye judge uprightly, O ye sons of men?
Yea, in heart ye work wickedness;
ye weigh the violence of your hands in the earth.

The wicked are estranged from the womb:
they go astray as soon as they be born,
speaking lies.

Their poison is like the poison of a serpent:
they are like the deaf adder that stoppeth her ear;
which will not hearken to the voice of charmers,
charming ever so wisely.

Break their teeth, O God, in their mouth:
break out the great teeth of the young lions, O Lord.
Let them melt away as waters which run continually:
when he bendeth his bow to shoot his arrows,
let them be as cut in pieces.

As a snail which melteth,

let every one of them pass away:
like the untimely birth of a woman,
that they may not see the sun.

Before your pots can feel the thorns,
he shall take them away as with a whirlwind,
both living, and in his wrath.

The righteous shall rejoice when he seeth the vengeance:
he shall wash his feet in the blood of the wicked.
So that a man shall say,
Verily there is a reward for the righteous:
verily he is a God that judgeth in the earth."

When he finished, his eyes remained close. No one spoke.
All sat in the contemplative lotus position around the dining
mat. No one dared recline. All food remained untouched.
Only wine was consumed.

Fully an hour passed before Jesus slowly opened his eyes.
He reached for a special drink the Beloved Disciple placed
before him hours before. He stood to speak to his most trusted
few. He took a loaf of bread, broke a piece for himself and
passed the remainder to his disciples, "Eat, for this is my
body." He lifted the wine glass that contained the special mix-
ture. "Drink, for this is my blood. Drink, because we must
drink no more until the New Kingdom is secure."

Jesus signaled Judas, "Go, you must perform the most
unpleasant task. May God go with you."

To Peter, Jesus repeated, "Peter, tonight you will betray
me thrice before the cock crows."

To all, he smiled and said, "Tonight is the end and the
beginning. We shall soon be together, again."

Death of Jesus

"Jesus, when he had cried again with a loud voice, yielded up the ghost."
        The Holy Bible, Matthew 27:50

The toast of blood complete, Jesus slowly set down the empty cup. He started to rise. The soft dining pillows and the wine made the attempt clumsy. His loved one quickly came to his feet and extended his arm to steady Jesus.

Jesus nodded thanks to Beloved Disciple and looked around the room. Gazing at each of the disciples, reclining still, he announced, "I must go now" with an air of foredoom. "Peter, James and John will come with me. You others, my lieutenants, gather as many of our followers as possible at this hour. You know where the seventy are. Come to the Gethsemane gardens. You must command our people to remain at the entrance to the large field of cabbages.[1] Romans will come. Do not attack the Romans or anger them in any way. We want only a show of force, no battle."

The disciples knew well the spot where Jesus would be found at a small clump of large rocks near the center of a field of mature cabbage. Jesus often went to that place to meditate and pray. The field's edge that Jesus warned his followers not to cross lay about eighty yards from the rocks.

"You should be there within the time it would take to drink a glass of wine. Remember, you must restrain and control our people. No matter what happens to me, do not fight. It is written, the Messiah must suffer alone. Save yourselves to fight another day and enjoy the coming Kingdom. Go with God. The Kingdom ruled by his law is at hand."

As the disciples arose to depart, Jesus did what seemed to be a strange thing. He touched Thomas the Twin gently on the shoulder. "Take this," handing Thomas his True Purple cloak, the badge of kingly authority. "Wear it at the appropriate time. You will know when."

Thomas, dumbfounded, slid the cloak under his robe, then followed the others downstairs into the busy streets.

The disciples spread out to collect supporters at pre-determined grouping positions. It was soon apparent, even to those few among the Passover throng that did not yet suspect a brewing insurrection, that something was astir. Judas hurried directly toward Fort Antonia.[2]

Judas Iscariot stood before the gates of Antonia. His head spun and his entire body shook at the awesome task before him. He loved Jesus like a brother. He would have given his own life to prevent the slightest harm to his life-long colleague. Now at the gate, he stood ready to demonstrate even more profoundly his love for Jesus. Judas would give not only his life, but also his honor and pride for the Righteous Teacher. He knew that his was an integral part of the conspiracy: to set the stage for what had to be done to carry out the Scriptures that promised a New Kingdom. Although it cut him deeply, he would obey the command of the Master no matter what the consequences. The gate guard questioned him.

"Who are you? Why would you disrupt the governor-general at this late hour?"

"I have important information. I can tell you where to capture the leader of the Nazarene insurrection."

"Why tonight? Why now?"

"The insurrection will be before dawn. The governor must act now."

"We will approach the governor."

Pontius Pilate instinctively knew that there was more to this report of insurrection than to the many he routinely received. He instructed the guard to begin the chain of events that would prepare the cohort for action. A cohort of about 600 fresh Roman soldiers were readied for the long-anticipated action.

Pilate prepared a letter of instruction to Herod. Since it was critically important to take every precaution to prevent a riot and general bloodshed, he wrote:

"Esteemed Herod,

I understand that the current leader of the Davidian movement, a fellow named Jesus, readies to submit himself to our mercy.

I have made ready a contingent of troops for your dispensation under the following stipulations: you must avoid contact between Roman troops and the local populace if at all possible. Our troops are available to prevent bloodshed, not cause it. All contact between rebel leaders must be made in the name of your Kingship, not Rome. I have dispatched a fine officer, Captain Malchus, to aid you in this matter. I suggest that you dispatch a small force headed by your most respected and accepted priestly authority to make the arrest. Again, both our futures depend upon a successful bloodless operation.[3]

Pilate"

Under escort, Judas carried the message to Herod. Herod seemed upset. "How am I to do this," he yelled to no one in particular. "He expects to find and arrest Jesus, to hear him before the Sanhedrin, present charges to Pilate for formal sentencing and quiet the people while the sentence is carried out. Doesn't he know that tomorrow night is the beginning of Passover? Any execution and burial must be complete before tomorrow night. It is now near midnight. Impossible! Impossible!"

"I shall have my reward, shall I not?" Judas suddenly seemed greedy.

"Yes, yes. Now sit there on the ground, low one. A man who would betray his comrades does not merit praise. My servants will organize a small police envoy to pick up Jesus. You, worm, must kiss the pretender to gain the reward."

Judas slumped to the ground and cried. Not only must he identify Jesus, he—Judas—must also die. Jesus had ordered him to take all necessary steps to avoid disclosing more details about the insurgent organization. This meant that he must take his own life so that he would not divulge secrets under the torture that was sure to come.

Jesus walked across the field toward the private refuge. A full moon, high overhead, lighted the area as if it were daylight. Jesus motioned for Peter and James to remain some distance from the rocks. They promptly lay down between the rows of cabbage, exhausted by the day's events. Jesus and his beloved Lazarus continued to the spot of peace. Since Jesus had given the True Purple cloak to Thomas, he and John Mark were clad the same. Their fine snow-white linen, glistened in the bright moonlight. Beloved Disciple tenderly helped his master to the spot where Jesus had so often lost himself in meditation.

Jesus knelt and talked to Abraham.[4] He must have prayed that the next three days would go as planned. One slip, one unforeseen occurrence could mean death for Jesus and the cause. Jesus knew that he was the chosen Messiah and thus had a predetermined destiny but he helped assure that destiny by careful planning and preparation. A magician did not rely upon chance to create illusion. The new King would not rely upon chance to fulfill the prognostications. Now, in that garden, though, it was time for faith and prayer. Jesus asked his Father to help him mobilize the scheme.

Jesus prayed intensely. Sweat poured from his brow. Some say his hands wrung in blood, yet his voice never carried beyond his beloved, who knelt beside him.

When Jesus finished, he arose and walked to the disciples Peter and James. They were asleep. He knew at that instant that in spite of all of his years of teaching, in spite of all of his vows of comradeship, proclaimed over the years since the days of their youthful gang, the disciples could not be fully trusted. He was truly alone.

Jesus bid the two disciples awaken and arise. No lanterns shone but Jesus still remained visible in the bright moonlight. Turning to his followers, now numbered in the hundreds, gathered at the edge of the field, he raised his arms and spoke. "Comrades, brothers in God, do not show your weapons. Do not speak. Remain motionless in place. See the lanterns at the city gate? They come now. It is I they seek and it is I alone the Scriptures say must suffer. After they take me, you must disperse into the countryside. I will return in three days and in due time will send instructions to you. The Kingdom is at hand."

Jesus fell silent. He did not move. The lanterns soon revealed a small group of about twenty Temple police, one priest, some Temple advisors and Captain Malchus. Behind them, in full battle gear, a cohort of foot soldiers clinked along without the aid of artificial lights.[5]

The Temple contingent made its way through the group of followers at the edge of the field. The authorities continued through the cabbage patch to a measured position facing Jesus, Peter, James and Beloved Disciple. The cohort stopped just past the followers to observe the proceedings at a distance. The Temple police, led by the priest with Malchus by his side, stopped no more than five feet from Jesus and the three lieutenants. They exchanged no words. A hooded man in the Temple group suddenly dropped his cover, exposing the stern face of Judas Iscariot. He stepped forward, walked directly to Jesus and, as if performing a ritual of death, kissed him on each cheek.

"Traitors," Malchus blurted.

"Death," Peter angrily responded. He drew his hidden sword in a continuous circular swinging motion and cut off the right ear of Malchus.

Jesus stepped forward before Malchus could respond. "Stop," he commanded. All froze. "You disobeyed my order. My command was no aggression whatsoever."

The Master reached down and picked up the bloody ear. He handed it to Malchus. "Put it back," he instructed. Puzzled, Malchus accepted the ear. Slowly he lifted it to his wound and held it there. "It is whole," said Jesus. Believing, Malchus dropped his arms. The ear remained, perfectly restored. No blood was present.

"I will go with you now to face what must be faced," Jesus said to Malchus and the priests. As he turned to go, Jesus instructed his followers one last time. "You must now disperse. Go into the world and spread the word." To his inductors he said, "Do not bind me. I will go as you direct. It is written."

The cabbage patch soon emptied. The cohort returned to the fort to guard against trouble. The followers of Jesus disappeared into the night. Peter and both James followed Jesus and the Temple police. The Beloved Disciple, John, slipped away to a newly chiseled sepulcher to prepare it for his master. The night was quiet.

As the band entered the city gates, Malchus stopped to order Jesus bound. He did not wish to leave the impression with the High Priest that Jesus controlled the proceedings.

The old priest, Annas, met the group at the Temple steps. Annas had accused Holy Mary and Joseph of illegal fornication in the conception of Jesus thirty-four years earlier in Galilee. He knew Jesus well and was no friend. Annas identified Jesus as the one who must stand trial.

James, half-brother of Jesus, took Jesus by the arm and the two sadly followed Annas up the stairs into the Temple. Simon Peter and the other James did not follow. The female gatekeeper asked Peter, "Do you not know Jesus? Would that you help and comfort him!"

Peter recoiled in fear. "I do not know this man. I was only passing by and stopped to join the excitement. I am not a disciple." Peter walked over to an open fire to warm himself alongside several Temple police.

The position of High Priest rotated among the members of the council. This year the council had voted Caiaphas to that honored and powerful position. Caiaphas was the Pharisee who long ago struck the boy Jesus and gained a withered hand. He was no friend of Jesus', either.

Pontius Pilate certainly sensed that there was a brewing insurrection in the air. Recent riots erupted when the Romans attempted to build a new aqueduct to service the fort.[6] Caiaphas conceived a scheme to pacify Roman concerns and keep his source of power.[7]

Caiaphas argued before the Council of High Priests that one Jewish political leader would have to be sacrificed to convince Pilate that the insurrection was repressed. The natural candidate for that honor fell to Barabbas who was clearly the leader of the aqueduct riots. He had been captured in the act of urging the rioters to storm the fort. Now he lay in chains, his fate the pleasure of Pontius Pilate.

Jesus provided Caiaphas another opportunity to test the plan. Caiaphas hated Jesus. Barabbas would likely cause no more trouble. Why not eliminate Jesus while pacifying Pilate?

Caiaphas sat as if in judgment of Jesus. In spite of the late hour, he wore the finest robes of the office of High Priest. Although this was no formal Sanhedrin meeting, some regular members of the Council attended.

Caiaphas spoke from his lofty chair overlooking the chained Jesus. "You claim to be the true king of Israel and Judea?"

"I am what I am."

"It is said that you plan to overthrow the government, expel the Romans and disband the Council. Would you be King, High Priest and Caesar? You stir up the passions of the people and make trouble for all of us. What say you for yourself?"

"I have taught openly. I have spoken in the Temple, in the courtyards, in the countryside Wheresoever people will listen, I have taught the word. I teach only what has been written since ancient times. I teach the truth. If the truth be wrong, how will this nation survive?"

"Do your followers need to be armed as if they were an army? We know that you demand much substance from those who would follow you. What do you do with so much material support?"

"There are many highwaymen. We receive only that which is God's."

Caiaphas fumed. Revenge would be his. "I know you well, Jesus of Galilee," he shouted. "You shall go before Pontius Pilate for sentencing as a conspirator against Caesar Tiberius. As for your blasphemy, you shall defile the name of our God no more after you die for treason."

There was no open disagreement among the members of the Council. They would lead Jesus to the fort and awaken Pontius Pilate to pronounce official judgment, the sacrifice offered in the person of Jesus.

Joseph of Arimathea sat as a member of council His eyes met those of Jesus in silent mutual understanding as Caiaphas announced his decision. It grieved Joseph to see Jesus condemned, but he had his orders. There was no turning back.

The first light of day glowed across the east wall as they led Jesus from the Temple to Fort Antonia. Caiaphas, Annas, Joseph of Arimathea and several members of the Council followed. At the outside gates of the fort, the priests stopped. It would be an unclean act to enter the walls on the day before Passover. Malchus, a non-Jew, led Jesus inside to face Pilate. After the gates closed behind them, as the light increased, a curious crowd began to gather around the priests of the Council. An hour passed with Jesus inside the walls of the fort.

Jesus and Malchus stood in the center of a large courtyard. Pilate walked out of the shadows alone, without escort. Raising his empty sword hand in a gesture of non-belligerence, he smiled and said, "Greetings. Greetings in the name of the Great Caesar, leader of men, conqueror of all the world, the benevolent and wise ruler of all people."

"And to you, may the single God smile upon your days," replied Jesus.

Faint smiles crossed the lips of each man, smiles of understanding at the gentle jousting of their salutes. Each spoke in the educated Greek dialect of the refined. The two men obviously respected each other.

"They claim that you have led an insurrection of the poor people, yet you are not one of them."

"I speak for all the people of Israel."

"Then you would be King?"

"What you have heard, so it is."

Pontius Pilate had no love for either King Herod or the Temple priestly authorities. To Pilate, it made no difference who was King or High Priest. His duty was to maintain order and collect tribute to help fund constant Roman military adventures. Whoever held the faith and trust of the people, helped collect taxes and prevented riots and rebellions that threatened the occupation would be acceptable to Pilate and to Rome.

The current king and priests were having problems maintaining civil order. Perhaps a change would be for the best.

Pilate had recently stripped some power from the indigenous administrators. He decreed that only the Roman governor, himself, had the authority to issue a death warrant to any man.[8] Of course, a woman found guilty of out-of-wedlock fornication evidenced by pregnancy would be stoned to death along with her unborn baby.[9] All other death warrants would be reviewed and approved by Pilate before being executed.

"Are you a Galilean?"

"I am a subject of the Kingdom of David, recently of Galilee," Jesus answered evasively.

Pilate tired of the conversation. "Herod Antipas, tetrarch of Galilee and Parae, is in residence here at the fort," Pilate noted. "Take the prisoner to him. If this man is a problem, it concerns only Herod. Jesus is no threat to Rome."

Malchus led Jesus away.

Herod Antipas showed no glee to see Jesus, though he had heard fascinating stories about the magical powers. "Show me some magic," snapped Herod Antipas. Jesus stood before him but would not speak. The scribes and attendants taunted Jesus with no response.

Furious, Herod ordered "Send him back to Pilate. Tell the Governor I find this man has plotted insurgency against Caesar. Tell him that he must die as a traitor."

Pilate, upset by the early morning political maneuvering, felt that the other two political entities (the king and the priests) sought to force any blame for the death of a popular leader upon his office. Any resultant public reaction would then be attributed to Roman occupiers. He resolved to block that perception.

When Jesus again arrived at the courtyard, Pilate led him to the main gate of the fort to face the priestly authorities and the swelling crowd just outside the walls. Raising his voice to address the crowd, he declared, "I find this man guilty of no crime. I have the authority to release him. It is the custom and the grace of Caesar to free one prisoner in honor of your Passover. Shall he be Jesus?"

"No! No!," shouted Caiaphas, echoed by the crowd.

"Release Barabbas. Release Barabbas," chanted the crowd.

"So be it," declared Pilate. "I do not know what harm this rabbi does. He cannot be King without the consent of the people. If people do not want him, why do you fear? If the people do want him and believe that he is King, then you cannot undo it."

"He is a threat to order. He would destroy the Temple. He would remake the priesthood. He must die," a priest answered.

Pilate turned toward his guards. "Release Barabbas. This man will take his place on the cross."

Pilate hoped that his action would alter the passions of the people. Caiaphas hoped that this sacrifice would restore power to him and to King Herod. Jesus hoped that his own plan would not fail. Pilate lifted a pitcher of water for all to see and poured it on his hands. "I wash my hands of this affair. You do what you wish with the 'King of the Jews.' I have dispatched a company of soldiers to help you."

The soldiers prepared Jesus for the march to the place of death: they scorned him with coarse, abusive and demeaning language. "The would-be King of the Jews, you are no more than a poor bastard. Your father is a northern barbarian and your mother a whore! You are nothing. We will laugh when you cry out in death."

They began the sad journey. The crowd pushed and shoved against the Roman escort. A new purple cape, not of the true royal brilliance, appeared across the shoulders of Jesus. Someone placed a crown fashioned of an olive branch upon his head. Jesus, upright, never appeared more majestic. The crowd dared not touch the King as the Roman Captain Malchus tried to interpret the wishes of Pilate.

Without orders, almost as if directed by some outside force, the soldiers began to escort Jesus through the city. A cross of execution prepared for Barabbas lay near the city gate. The soldiers grew uneasy. A person of the social rank of Jesus should not be required to carry an object as heavy as the cross, yet it was the custom that the condemned carry his own instrument of death. An unlikely volunteer stepped forward to solve the problem.

A dark-skinned foreigner pushed through the guards and lifted the cross onto his shoulders.[10] He spoke Greek to Jesus. Jesus nodded acknowledgment. Jesus recognized the man as Simon of Cyrene. Cyrene was a Greek outpost in north Africa that traded grain, oil, horses, and medicinal ingredients with Israel and Judea via the port city of Tyre. Simon was the successful broker of silphium laciniatum that Thomas the Twin contacted on his quick trip to Tyre. Simon played a dangerous game appearing in Jerusalem at that time. He was one of the very few who knew the secret of the drug that simulated death. His physical appearance clearly marked him as a foreigner and gentile out of place in a Jewish city during holy days. More perilous, he was a long-time business acquaintance of the dyer Jesus and had a vested interest in Jesus' scheme.

The procession worked its way along the north wall of the quarter called Suburb, out of the northwest gate and down the road toward the village of Emmaus. Soon, Jesus was leading the entire group with a quick, determined cadence. In short time they reached the place of death, a hill called Golgotha Place of the Skulls. Simon dropped the cross. The Roman guards prepared Jesus for the ordeal. The large crowd that had followed was suddenly mostly absent. It was mid-morning.

The guards took the purple cloak. Jesus remained loosely draped in white linen. He saw his feet and hands nailed to the cross. The guards hoisted the cross upright and dropped its base into an already dug hole. To the cross the guards attached a sign that Pilate had written in three languages identifying Jesus as 'King of the Jews.'[11] Here was no ordinary criminal nor just a teacher whose words offended religious sensitivities. Here was the royal child of David, the man who would be King of the Jews.

On each side of the cross upon which Jesus hung was a highway robber: One was Titus and the other Dumachus,[12] the leaders of the band of robbers that had waylaid Joseph, Mary and baby Jesus so many years past. They had suffered on the crosses since the evening before and were still alive. The robbers knew Jesus and remembered his power as an infant. They asked, "Why do you not save yourself? We know you have the power to do so."

"I must first die before we all shall live," Jesus replied. This seemed a strange contradiction to the robbers. No more was said.

Several women wailers dressed in black mourned near the execution site. Among those who wept for Jesus were four Mary's. One was his mother, Holy Mary. One was Mary

Magdalene who, as a woman, admired and loved Jesus. Another was Mary of Bethany. The fourth Mary was the first wife of Joseph and mother of Jesus' half-brothers and half-sisters, now wife of Cleophas. This last was the poor soul that Salomé Herod and her husband, Zebedee, had forced to conceive with Zebedee and be surrogate mother of Salomé's two children. These women, each named Mary, remained during the entire crucifixion process.[13]

The soldiers retired a few yards from the crosses. While they rested upon the ground they talked, gambled, and awaited the death of their clientele.

Jesus began to chant a psalm that had been written by King David during the days of plenty and happiness: 'A Cry of Anguish and Song of Praise.' "My God, my God, why hast thou forsaken me? Why art thou so far from helping me and from the words of my roaring?"

No doubt, some that heard these words and did not know their source thought Jesus despondent, but he only repeated familiar words that many believed promised the return of Davidian rule.

The psalm addressed the charge that Jesus, as Messiah, should save himself from execution, "He trusted on the Lord that he would deliver him, seeing he delighted in him."

"...the assembly of wicked have enclosed me: they pierced my hands and my feet. I may tell all my bones: they took and stare upon me.[14] They part my garments among them and cast lots upon my vesture."[15]

Jesus stopped. A small group of men had gathered near the cross. These were the intended burial detail from the house of Joseph of Arimathea. As planned, Joseph, using his influence as a well respected and trusted member of the Temple Council, obtained permission from Pontius Pilate to take the body of Jesus, when it appeared depleted of life, to an already prepared burial vault. But first the guards must see Jesus as dead.

At first, the men thought Jesus unconscious, then he spoke, "I thirst." This was the signal to give Jesus the drug that would make him appear dead, the drink from Tyre that his father, Joseph, lover John Mark, and grandfather, Joachim, had used so advantageously. The drink was hoisted to Jesus' lips by a long pole. He drank and continued the psalm. It praised the God of Israel and promised victory over her enemies. "For the

Kingdom is the Lord's: he is the governor among the nations."
The guards noticed the treasonous statement. One leapt to his
feet, angry that a Jew would proclaim independence from Caesar and Rome. "Let him finish," a comrade pleaded.

Jesus continued, his speech weaker and slurred. "They
shall come and shall declare his righteousness unto a people
that shall be born, that he hath done this." This pronounce-
ment that a truly God-directed theocracy would rule the land of
David completed the psalm. Jesus said, "It is finished." He
spoke no more.

Silence overwhelmed the place of the skulls. On the left
and on the right of Jesus, the two highwaymen slumped in
acceptance of death. Darkness engulfed the land. Some say the
earth shook. Others say that the curtain in the Temple, the curtain that Holy Mary had dyed, mysteriously split in the middle.
Still others saw angels descend from heaven. Even the women
mourners stayed silent. For three hours (from twelve o'clock
until three in the afternoon), stillness prevailed.

At about three, the Roman guards grew concerned. Of the
three men suffering on crosses, only Jesus appeared to be completely dead.[16] Jewish law required that all be buried before the
day of Passover began at sunset in the evening and Pontius
Pilate had ordered that the law be respected. The guards
decided to use a tested and proven method to hurry the expira-
tion of the two highwaymen. They crushed the legs of each with
a heavy hammer. This stopped the heart and produced almost
instant death.

Because he appeared dead, Jesus evaded the hammer. The
guard who had been so antagonized by the words of the psalm
would not allow the burial detail to remove Jesus' body until he
released some of his anger on it. The guard thrust his lance
deep into the side of Jesus. The comatose body of Jesus bled
freely, proving that he still lived. The drug had worked perfectly. All who saw Jesus thought him dead. Except for the
action of one soldier, Jesus' scheme to stage his own death and
return to overthrow the triad government could have come to
fruition. The soldier's lance changed history.

Jesus died from the wound.

Fini

"After this, they asked them what they had seen; who answered with one accord, In the presence of the God of Israel we affirm, that we plainly saw Jesus talking with his disciples in Mount Olivet, and ascending up to heaven."

The Lost Books, 'Nicodemus' 12:7

The corpse of Jesus was carefully removed from the cross by the servants of Joseph. Without ceremony, the Messiah was gently rolled into white linen and carried by six large men to the pre-arranged burial vault. There it would rest horizontally on a bed of down and linen. Only the rich and royal were afforded a burial of this nature. The thieves, Titus and Dumachus, were given the burial of the poor. They were dropped into deep holes just large enough for one vertical body each and covered with earth. The soldiers dragged the highwaymen to their final resting place.

The small man-made cave that held the body of Jesus was not intended to be his final destination. The facilities there were certainly worthy of any prince, but Jesus should not have been dead. After the drug's effects had subsided in about three days, Jesus was to leave the sepulcher and lead the insurgency as the promised Messiah. This didn't happen.

Only two persons followed the burial party to the sepulcher. One was the disciple Mary Magdalene, filled with fantasies of everlasting complete union of her body with that of Jesus. Hers was much more than common sexual imagery. She imagined a sort of vague uniting of bodies and souls into one in which she would absorb the essence of Jesus' love and insight. She felt that if at one time her body had been possessed by demons and evil spirits, why should not the spirit of Jesus enter her as had the demons but endow her with peace and understanding, not hurt and hate? Mary Magdalene deeply wished she could join Jesus in death; lacking that, she just wanted to be near her healer and teacher.

Mary, mother of Jesus, did not follow the burial procession. Instead, she accompanied John, the beloved disciple, to his home in the Essene quarter of Jerusalem. There she would rest, grieve and contemplate recent events until her death a few years later. She never understood why Jesus had rejected her love and embraced the multitude. It was she who convinced Jesus he was the Messiah come to reclaim the land of David for the pious and the righteous. It was she who introduced Jesus to the classic teaching of the rich and refined. It was she who taught Jesus the True Way of the Essene sect. Why had he abandoned her in his final years? Even as he died on the cross, Jesus did not acknowledge his mother's presence. She would never understand how commitment to a cause could negate the ties of family and love of a mother.

Mary of Bethany returned home to her family after Jesus was taken from the cross. She was certain Jesus was dead, but later events would convince her otherwise.

Mary, mother of Jesus' half-brothers and half-sisters and the surrogate mother for Salomé was fascinated by the day's events. She had not known Jesus as a child or as the insurgency leader, but she had profound hopes for the movement's success. After all, she was the mother of five of its leaders. James the Lesser, Simon, and Judas were fathered by Joseph and James Boanerges and John Boanerges were sired by Salomé's husband. Her hatred of the Herod kingship was magnified by her longing for a return of the Davidian dynasty. She and Mary Magdalene sat wake outside the tomb of Jesus.

The servants of Joseph of Arimathea placed the linen-clad body of Jesus on a shelf that had been chiseled out of the stone wall of the tomb. The pure white linen stood in sharp contrast to the cold, damp walls of the vault. Jesus was at rest within the still open vault only a few minutes before sunset.

At sunset the new day began. The new day had special significance for those under Jewish law. It was the day of the unleavened bread, Passover. The festival of Passover commemorated the exodus of the Israelite people from slavery 2,000 years earlier. The heavy black cloud that had darkened the day as Jesus died on the cross continued to block celestial light. After sunset, it was very, very dark.

Passover began before the burial party could close the tomb. To move the heavy rock over the tomb opening would have been prohibited labor under the law. Thus the tomb remained open from the beginning of Passover at sunset until the end of the Sabbath at sunset two days later. In spite of the open tomb and the special festival, however, much activity clustered around the burial site for the next twenty-four hours.

In the dark night, two disciples separately made their way to the tomb. Neither used artificial light for guidance: they feared the Pharisees with their strict interpretation of the law would condemn this activity if they were betrayed by lanterns. One disciple was Nicodemus and the other was John.

Nicodemus struggled along carrying a heavy bag. The bag contained fine imported herbs and body oils. Nicodemus sprinkled myrrh inside the tomb and on the body of Jesus. He lovingly and reverently moistened Jesus' face with aloe. When he finished, he left the remainder of the cargo within the tomb. What remained looked a lot like medical supplies. Nicodemus quietly slipped back into the city.

John 'Lazarus' was the other disciple to visit the vault. John had helped Holy Mary to his home, cleansed and anointed himself, dressed in the finest snow-white linens and returned to the tomb after the burial party arrived with the body of Jesus. Within the vault, John watched over his beloved.

As the sun rose on the day of Passover, Annas and Caiaphas worried about the consequences of the crucifixion. Would it make Jesus a martyr, his followers attempting an overthrow of the priestly government in spite of his death? A chill came over their conversation as Annas spoke, "The followers of Jesus, they understand the Scriptures of our ancestors as predicting a supernatural resurrection of the Messiah?"

"I know of what they speak," answered Caiaphas. "I have studied the Scriptures to which they refer. I cannot, in my heart of hearts, find anything in those words of which they speak that would predict a Messiah that recovers from death."

"If they believe, it is of no importance what is written. What they perceive is real."

"You speak wise words, but why do you fret over silly superstitions of the peasants? Jesus is dead. He will not rise up from the dead and be king of those people!"

Annas showed his advanced age as well as his keen intellect. He put his right arm around the shoulders of Caiaphas to sturdy himself. He whispered in the ear of the High Priest, "What if the disciples steal the body and claim it to be ascended up into heaven? You know the people! The more bizarre the story the more likely they will believe it. If the story that Jesus has come back from the dead is circulated, it will only be days before thousands will claim—and themselves believe—that they have seen him."

"And the insurgents will rule in the name of a Holy Jesus."

"Yes."

"We must stop this nonsense before it begins. I will ask Pilate to dispatch a troop of soldiers to guard the sepulcher. The body of Jesus will rot in that cold, dark place where it belongs. It will return to dirt like the blasphemy that he advocated," Caiaphas declared. He thought for a moment and continued to outline a strategic plan. "And, we will begin to arrest and condemn the disciples just as soon as the passions of the people subside. We must totally rid ourselves of this cancer."

A messenger from Caiaphas soon arrived at Fort Antonia. She relayed the request for guards for the tomb to Pontius Pilate. He quickly responded positively.

Centurion Petronius was selected to head the guard operation. If security of the body was the objective, the choice could not have been worse. Since first accepting the faith of the Jews and Jesus as their true leader that day two years ago in Capernaum, Centurion Petronius' faith and covert commitment had intensified. He was less than enthusiastic about performing any duty that might hurt the cause.

Petronius personally led the first detail to the burial site. He selected a repose along the only path to the tomb against a large overhanging rock. It was mid-day. The rock offered the only shade from the hot sun. Perhaps out of respect for the dead but more likely out of purposeful neglect of duty, Petronius did not order any soldier to inspect the tomb. The rock shelter prevented direct observation of the tomb.

The soldiers were soon engaged in a noon meal. Any responsibility to actually watch the tomb was taken lightly. Some food and much wine was consumed. Soon, each soldier was either groggily resting or deep asleep within the cool shade.

The tomb was still open. Simon Peter joined John within its confines. Peter simply walked around the would-be guards when he noticed them lying beneath the rock.

The sun set. It was now the day of rest, the Sabbath, the start of the second day of the internment of Jesus.

The guards awoke at sunrise with the sun's rays blasting against the rock. With the morning sun it would be uncomfortable to remain in the position that had been so well selected the previous afternoon. As the guards moved to the opposite side of the rock, they noticed the large rock door to the sepulcher had not yet been closed. Embarrassed of his earlier inattention, Petronius ordered his charges to quickly push the heavy rock door closed. In their haste, the guards did not investigate inside the vault. Petronius ordered seven seals be affixed to the stone door to detect any opening of it. On each seal he wrote the previous day's date.

As the sun passed overhead the guard detail returned to the east side of the rock. There they pitched a tent and prepared an evening meal. More cautious than the day before, Petronius selected two soldiers to remain on the west side of the rock and guard the very entrance of the sepulcher.

The two soldiers sat on the ground with their backs against the rock door. After sunset the third day they dozed. A fearful thing happened. The door to the sepulcher slowly opened. Awakened by the movement, the guards ran a few yards and stopped. The fear of losing their lives for desertion equaled the fear of ghosts. They looked back at the tomb in terror. They could neither run nor return. They later testified that they heard a loud voice from heaven that was not heard by the main guard contingent camped twenty yards away. Three men emerged from the tomb. One was carried limply between the other two, his feet dragging in the dust. The soldiers, frozen in place, could not stop the slow escape of the three.

A few minutes later, as they regained their composure, the two soldiers looked at each other. They considered what to do. An explanation would have to be collaborated between the two. The more terrifying the story told to their superiors the less likely severe punishment would be administrated.

The soldiers decided to wake Centurion Petronius and relate an astonishing tale to him. In addition to the loud voice, they told of two angels descending from the heavens, rolling the rock away and carrying Jesus upward toward a bright heavenly light. For good measure they related how dead men had burst out of their graves and been sucked upward beyond sight, the ground shook and the cross of Jesus spoke and the heavens answered. Undaunted by the preposterousness of this story, Petronius believed and hurriedly withdrew the entire guard detail to consult with Pilate.

Pilate also believed the story. Centurion Petronius convinced him a miracle had occurred. He proclaimed that he was guiltless in the death of Jesus, but he feared that Jesus might still be alive and not be so quick to judge him innocent. It was best, thought Pilate, that no other person know what had happened at the tomb that night, therefore he ordered the centurion and the soldiers to say nothing.

Mary Magdalene and the small group of women she assembled arrived at the burial site the next morning, the first day of the new week. As expected, they found the door open, but not as wide as when Mary had last seen it.

In addition to Mary Magdalene, several other notable women were in the wailing party. One was Mary, mother of Zebedee's children. Another was Joanna, wife of King Herod's personal steward, Chuza. Mary, mother of Jesus, was not in the group.

As the women approached the sepulcher, the sun shined through the door opening. It became more and more apparent that Jesus was not lying in the prepared place. The sun cast direct rays on some burial linens that were draped over two walking sticks leaning against the vault's rock face. To the women, these bright linens appeared as divine -- angels. All the women except Mary Magdalene fled in terror.

Mary knelt beside the open door and cried, "They have taken him. They have taken him. Why? Why? They would not even grant us the right to give him a proper funeral. Cruel..... Evil....." She fell face down in the dust and rock and wept.

Through her sorrow and anger Mary sensed the presence of another person. She looked up to see a dark, hooded figure near her. "Where have you carried him?" she asked. "Tell me and I will take him far away."

"Do you not know me, Mary?" the hooded person asked in a deep monotone voice.

"Mary," she repeated to herself. He knows me. Mary then recognized the hood and cape. It was the unique True Purple cloak of Jesus. Mary didn't know that Jesus had given the cloak to Thomas the Twin after his last supper.

"The coat....You are Jesus," Mary exclaimed in amazed joy. "You live."

Mary reached out to touch the man, but he quickly drew away. "Do not touch Me. I have not yet transcended this life. There is much to do before I ascend to meet our God."

Mary rushed to tell the other disciples that she had seen and spoken to Jesus. She found them in the upstairs room of John's house plotting for the immediate future. On one point they all agreed; the movement would have to move underground for an indefinite period of time. It was too dangerous, the passions of the people too inflamed, the authorities too alert to press the issues at this time.

In the stillness of the upper room, all doors bolted from the inside and windows closed and locked, the disciples reflected in silence. A bioluminescent glow appeared in the middle of the room. As the amazed disciples watched, the glow formed an image of Jesus. The image spoke, "Peace be with you. As I have been sent by my father, so I command you to go into the countryside, hide, preach the truth of the Kingdom of David wherever you go. Time is on our side. We shall prevail."

The image of Jesus faded. A cool breeze filled the room; as it touched each disciple he felt the presence of the Holy Ghost. One reporter has said the voice of Jesus was heard to say, "You now receive the Holy Ghost."

Thomas the Twin was not in the room when the materialization of Jesus appeared. Eight days later a meeting of the disciples included Thomas. This time Jesus appeared as a normal man. When Thomas expressed doubt that this man was Jesus, Jesus invited him to inspect the nail punctures in his hands and lance wound in his side. Thomas believed.

The body of Jesus was never found. As King Herod Archelaus feared, reports of Jesus appearances surfaced all over the area. Jesus was seen on the road to Emmaus not far from the execution site. He appeared to the disciples in the hide-out cave in Galilee. He even helped Peter and Andrew find fish on an otherwise unlucky day. Many saw him, but he did not tarry long at any one place. It took another miracle to quiet the ghost of Jesus and put him to rest until another day.

The disciples gathered for one last time—some say at Mary's home in Bethany. Jesus lifted his arms and blessed the disciples, commanded them to go separate ways and teach the revolution. With his arms still outstretched, he slowly began to ascend up into heaven. As he faded from sight his essence followed his body.

So it is said.

Endnotes

Chapter 1: Mother of Jesus

[1] *C.E.* (or *Common Era*) refers to the term most historians now use to describe the Christian era.

[2] *Genesis* 37:25. ".......behold, a company of Ishmaelites came from Gilead with their camels bearing spicery and balm and myrrh, going to carry it down to Egypt." There are numerous references to the camel in Biblical writings. The reader should note that the camel seems to have been so much a part of everyday life that authors often assumed the reader would know the important part camel transportation played in many stories. Only the very poor walked cross-country.

[3] *Ezekiel* 27:1-10. Ezekiel describes with some detail the complexity of the Tyre sailing ship and some logistics involved in gathering its components. Some scholars speak of ship trade as distant as the British Isles during the time of Jesus.

[4] *Chronicles* 2:1-18, *1 Kings* 5:1-17, *Ezra* 3:7.

[5] *Genesis* 30:1-21. The drug mentioned was mandrake. Mandrake is known for its narcotic and emetic properties. Here it is claimed to induce fertility.

[6] *Matthew* 1:3-16. A detailed, if not very convincing, genealogy.

[7] *Luke* 2:36-38. Also, *Lost Books of the Bible*, "The Birth of Mary."

[8] *Deuteronomy* 33:1-29, *Genesis* 49:20, *Ruth* 4:18-22, *II Samuel* 2:1-7, and some recent scholars.

[9] *Numbers* 2:27, 26:46-47, *Judges* 5:17.

[10] *II Chronicles* 30:11. Chaim Potok discusses YHWH in *Wanderings*.

[11] "The Birth of Mary," Chapter 1. Much of the story related in this chapter is found in two books of the so-called *Lost Books of the Bible*. I have depended heavily upon "The Birth of Mary" and "The Protevangelion" in telling the story of Mary and her parents. Please read my "Introduction" for remarks concerning these sources. I will not attempt to reference these sources in every instance in this and Chapter Two.

[12] Herod the Great was installed by Rome as King of Israel and Judea about 37 B.C. He could prove no royal lineage acceptable to the Jews.

The Herod clan was actually Idumaean. As the Herod family ruled at the pleasure of Rome, so the priests ruled in matters of law at the pleasure of the Herods. Thus, 'puppet of the puppets.'

[13] The 'Righteous Teacher' was an essential facet of the Essene sect beliefs. I will argue that Jesus was a product of Essene thought if not an acknowledged member of the sect. I am not alone in this perception: *Morals and Dogma of Freemasonry*, Albert Pike, The Supreme Council of the Southern Jurisdiction, Charleston 1871, reprinted by L.H. Jenkins, Richmond, 1921, page 260: "He (Christ) never once mentioned the Essenes, between whose doctrines and his there was so great a resemblance, and in so many points, so perfect an identity."

Also see *Jesus and the Dead Sea Scrolls*, ed. James Charlesworth, "Jesus, the Primitive Community, and the Essene Quarter of Jerusalem," Rainer Riesner, Doubleday, 1993. In *The Dead Sea Scrolls and the Christian Myth*, John M. Allegro, Prometheus Books, New York, 1984, suggests Jesus was the Righteous Teacher and the New Testament is a myth that grew out of Essene beliefs.

[13] Qumran is not specified in *The Lost Books of the Bible* as the place Joachim and Anna sent Mary. Mary spent her youth in Qumran, the holy center of Essene learning, or the Essene quarter in Jerusalem. Qumran seems most probable.

[14]*Luke* 1:26-35. "And when she saw him,..."

The Koran, Mary 19:12. "We sent to her Our spirit in the semblance of a full-grown man. And when she saw him, she said, 'May the merciful defend me from you! If you fear the Lord, leave me and go your way.'

"I am the messenger of your Lord," he replied, "and have come to give you a holy son."

The Book of Mormon, Alma 7:10. Also *Nephi* 11:13-20. "And he said to me: Behold, the virgin whom thou seest is the mother of the Son of God, after the manner of the flesh."

Religious texts agree that there was something very earthly in the spirit that visited Mary.

Chapter 2: Joseph

[1] The story of the selection of Joseph is related in *The Lost Books of the Bible*, "The Protevangelion," Chapter Eight. Most of the story in this chapter relates to that source.

[2] *Matthew* 1:16. Matthew's genealogy makes Joseph the son of a contemporary Jacob, suggesting that our Joseph's life and background are akin to the ancient Joseph and his father, Jacob. Luke's genealogy of Joseph (*Luke* 3:23-38) differs completely from Matthew's, however.

[3] The phrase "Son of God" in Essene means much the same as "Brother in God" in other sects. It did not mean "Born of God." See *Jesus and the Dead Sea Scrolls*, James Charlesworth, ed., "Recovering Jesus' Formative Background," Paolo Sacchi, Doubleday, 1992, page 131.

[4] Zealots were active, organized and armed insurgents who fought against Roman occupation. The Zealots later became part of the Davidian organization planned here by the Qumran priests and later led by Jesus and Peter. A known active Zealot would have imposed much too great a burden on secrecy to be selected as the husband of Mary.

[5] *Webster's New Twentieth Century Dictionary*, Simon & Schuster, New York, 1979 defines one meaning of rod "...in Biblical use, an offshoot or branch of a family or tribe; stock or race; as, the 'rod of Isaiah.'"

Rod as a family tree is used in the *King James Version of the Holy Bible*, Exodus 4:20, "Moses carried the rod of God back to Egypt."

David ruled by divine right: *Psalms* 110:2, "The Lord shall send the rod of thy strength out of Zion: rule thou in the midst of thine enemies."

[6] As prophesied in *Isaiah* 11:1-2, "And there shall come forth a rod out of the stem of Jesse, and a branch shall grow out of his roots: And the spirit of the Lord shall rest upon him, the spirit of wisdom and understanding, the spirit of counsel and might, the spirit of knowledge and the fear of the Lord..."

[7] *Judges* 8:26, *Luke* 16:19, *Acts* 16:14. Webster's defines purple as "...in ancient times, crimson cloth or clothing, especially as an emblem of royalty or high rank."

[8] This story from the *Protevangelion* occurs in other texts devoted to the God of Abraham. The power of the dove was predicted by *Hosea* 11:11, "They shall tremble as a bird out of Egypt, and as a dove out of the land of Assyria.

[9] *Isaiah* 7:1-25 details the war, its horrible results and the coming of the Messiah/ruler out of its ashes. Modern preachers often quote this passage to forecast the end of all time. Clearly, Isaiah was simply predicting a very likely occurrence that would happen in about the next fifty years.

[10] *Jesus: A Life*, Wilson, pages 76-77

[11] The many names of our subject is due primarily to the many written translations through many languages. *Yesha* or *Joshua* would be his given name in Hebrew. *Jesus* is a Greek language corruption of *Yesha*. Only *Isaiah* called Him *Immanuel* or God. *Christ* is a Greek word for Messiah and can be translated as King or Ruler. We'll call little *Yesha* Jesus.

[12] In addition to the Lost Books "Protevangelion" account, this incident is related in The Koran, "Imrans" 3:40, "The angels said to Mary 'God bids you rejoice in a word from him. His name is Messiah, Jesus the son of Mary'." The Book of Mormon, "Mosiah" 3:8 says, "And he shall be called Jesus Christ, the Son of God, the Father of heaven and earth, the creator of all things from the beginning; and his mother shall be called Mary."

[13] More about this nitrite-benzene type product in later chapters.

[14] *The Messianic Legacy*, Baigent, Leigh and Lincoln, Dell, New York, 1989, pages 60-63. My intent here was not to suggest complete celibacy on the part of the Essene lay population.

Chapter 3: Birth and Infancy

[1] "An overwhelming body of evidence indicates that Nazareth did not exist in Biblical times." *The Messianic Legacy*, Baigent, Leigh and Lincoln, Dell Publishing, New York, 1989, page 30.

[2] Again, much of the story related in this chapter can be found in *The Lost Books of the Bible*, "Infancy of Jesus Christ" and "The Protoevangelion." Speculation about these books not being included in the *Holy Bible* can be found in the introductory remarks.

[3] No such summons has been found in written Roman records. It was ignored by Mark and John. However, this myth is essential to the basic idea that Jesus as Messiah had to be born in Bethlehem. *Luke* 2:1, *Matthew* 2:6.

[4] Isaiah, of course, did not envision the Roman Empire. He did, however, predict a terrible war with Assyria. Here I depict the old man ignoring how Isaiah had very specifically named the nation with which Israel would fight and win. He was not alone. Millions of apocalyptic preachers as well as New Testament writers have followed the example of the old man and pretended that the ancient writers were predicting much more than the words they wrote. *Isaiah* 7:10-23.

[5] *Matthew* 2:2.

[6] *Lost Books of the Bible*, "Infancy," Chapter One. Note the birth was depicted as occurring outside the limits of Bethlehem. Perhaps this is one reason this text was rejected by the council of Nice.

[7] It is difficult for the author to believe that the wise men were so unwise as to betray the baby Jesus. Only two accounts can be readily found that they did: *Matthew* 2:1-12, and Infancy 4:1,2. The wise men from Qumran most surely had calculated a convergence of three stars.

[8] *Matthew* 2:16. It is significant that Herod ordered all children to be killed. This indicates that his contemporaries believed that the Messiah could have been either male or female.

[9] *Matthew* 2:13-15. This story is not mentioned in *Luke, Mark* or *John*. It is detailed in *Infancy*. The entire idea seems to be linked to Joseph, the pre-exile ancestor of Jesus (*The Koran*, "Joseph").

[10] *Matthew* 23:35. Also discussed in notes of the 1979 printing of *The Lost Books of the Bible*, p. 36-37.

[11] The Sea of Reeds, sometimes referred to as the Sea of Weeds, was the sea that God opened for fleeing Israelis in the story of Moses. It is not the Red Sea we know today. See *Exodus* 14:21-31, also *Wanderings*, Chaim Potok, Fawcett: New York, 1988. p.100-101.

[12] There is no known written description of Jesus' physical appearance. My guess is that it was unique. The rumor that Jesus' father was from the region we now know as Europe (see Chapter Two notes) may give cause to speculate that his eyes were blue. Certainly, his head was shaved to fulfill the prophecies of *Isaiah* 9. Fifteen years after Jesus' death, Paul wrote "Doth not even nature itself teach you if a man have long hair, it is a shame unto him?" *Corinthians* 11:14. The Middle Ages custom of long

hair is reflected in paintings of that era. Short hair was the custom of Jesus' time. See *Isaiah* 7:20, *I Corinthians* 11:14.

[13] In addition to being related in *Infancy*, this story can be found also in *The Koran*, "Mary" 19:29. Newborn Jesus also spoke to Mary to help her understand his holy birth (*The Koran*, "The Table" 5:110). God Said, "Jesus, son of Mary, remember the favor I have bestowed on you and your mother: how I strengthened you with the Holy Spirit, so that you preached to men *in your cradle* and in the prime of manhood."

[14] *Jesus the Magician*, Norton Smith, Barnes & Noble: New York, 1993.

[15] The story of John can be found in many sources. In addition to the Lost Books mentioned earlier, some other sources are The Koran, "Mary" 19:1-22; "The Prophets" 21:88; "The Imrans" 3:37-47; and in the Holy Bible: *Matthew* 3:3-4, 11:16-18, 14:3-12; *Luke* 1:11-20, 3:1-3; *John*:29-36, 5:33, 3:25-31; *Mark* 1:1-8, 6:20. *Luke* 1:13, "But the angel said to him (Zechariah), 'Fear not, Zechariah, for thy prayer is at hand; and thy wife Elizabeth shall bear thee a son, and thou shalt call his name John.'"

Chapter 4: Youth

[1] *The Lost Books* record this myth as well as others in this chapter. Professor Henry Sike first translated the Lost Books myth at Cambridge University in 1697. Gnostic sect members who were followers of Jesus Christ purportedly used the text. Because much of this relatively long text resides in material published for other groups of common believers, material such as *Morals and Dogma* of the Freemasons and the *Koran* of the Muslims, it is most assuredly old text and I accept it as authentic.

[2] *Mark* 6:3 and *Matthew* 13:55 list the names of the brothers and indicates that there were at least two sisters. These are the natural children of Joseph and his first wife Mary.

[3] Many scholars conclude that Judas was a full brother of Jesus. The story of a Judas being cured by Jesus is found in *Infancy*. That he might have remained with the family of Jesus after this incident is my explanation of why they might have appeared as brothers. Note that Jesus also had a half-brother named Judas or 'Jude.'

[4] A boy of twelve would be tested by the temple authorities for possible priestly potential. This is one of the very few glances of the life of a young Jesus in the authorized versions of his life. *Luke 2:41-50*.

Chapter 5: Dye Shop Conspiracy

[1] *Jesus and the Riddle of the Dead Sea Scrolls*, Barbara Thiering, Harper, San Francisco, 1988 edition, pp. 44-48. *The Dead Sea Scrolls and the Christian Myth*, John Allegro, Prometheus, Buffalo, 1992 edition, pp. 114-119.

[2] Doctrines and practices of pre-Christian pagan, Jewish and early Christian sects who believed that secret knowledge could secure release for the soul from imprisonment in the material body.

[3] From *The Lost Books* and other readings, I find evidence that Jesus was a skilled craftsman, "carpenter," that dyed cloth. I selected Tiberias as a likely place for a new shop because the city was new and because several disciples lived and worked nearby. It would have been awkward for them to travel to Nazareth and study under Jesus while still engaged in commercial enterprise along the Sea of Galilee.

[4] *Holy Bible*, Gold Seal Edition, Royal Publishers, Nashville, 1966, page 309. I relate the story of a childhood incident involving Bartholomew and Jesus in Chapter Four.

[5] The story of childhood companionship is explained in Chapter Four. The Royal Publishers *Holy Bible*, page 310, also recounts the story in detail. Judas Iscariot is perhaps the most enigmatic of all the Jesus disciples. He generates much speculation and interest among Biblical authors including the myth of his betrayal of Jesus.

[6] *Holy Bible*, Royal Publishers, page 309. *The Death of Jesus*, Joel Carmichael, Horizon, New York, 1982, page 66. *Jesus: A Revolutionary*, John Dominic Crossan, Harper, San Francisco, 1989 edition, pp. 133-136. *Mark 15:40* offers thin evidence but this scenario makes sense in an attempt to reconstruct a coherent chain of events. See also *Matthew 13:55-57, Jude (Judas) 1, Galatians 1:19*.

[7] *Mark 6:3* and *Acts 1:13* indicate that he was a brother of James the Younger. See also the *Holy Bible*, Royal Publishers, p. 310.

[8] *Holy Bible*, Royal Publisher, p. 311. *Luke 6:13-16, 5:1-9. Jesus*, Crossan, p. 166-7. *What the Bible Really Says*, Manfred Barthel, Quill, New York, 1983, pp. 307, 315 and 329. Peter wrote the *Gospel of Mark* and the *First Epistle of Peter*, He met Jesus when very young.

[9] *Holy Bible*, Royal Publishers, page 309. Andrew is often mentioned with Simon Peter. Andrew was an early disciple of John the Baptist, *John 1:40* and *Luke 6:14*.

[10] James and John were called sons of Zebedee. *Matthew 4:21-22, Mark 3:17*. Zebedee was the husband of Salomé. *Smith's Bible Dictionary*, p. 581. Mary was the mother of James and John. *Matthew 27:56*: "...Mary the mother of James and Joses (John) and the mother of Zebedee's children."

[11] *Holy Bible*, Royal Publishers, p.31. *John 1:43-51, Matthew 10:3, Mark 3:18* and *Luke 6:14*.

[12] Simon Zelote (the Zealot) was a central force in the insurgency. *The Messianic Legacy*, Baigent, Leigh & Lincoln, Dell, New York, 1989, pp. 50-52. *The Dead Sea Scrolls*, Allegro, pp. 140-147. *Matthew 10:4*. Possibly a half-brother of Jesus, *Matthew 13:55*. He attempted to continue the Messiahship after the death of Jesus, *Acts 8:9-25*.

[13] Thomas the Twin, or Judas Thomas, was rumored to have been the twin brother of Jesus by many living during the Renaissance. Baigent, Leigh & Lincoln present the birth twin argument in *Messianic Legacy*,

pp. 94-99. Thomas may have so resembled Jesus that many thought they were twins. *Thomas* translated from the Aramaic means *twin*, but the Bible does not hint that Thomas was a birth twin. Note that *twin* also means "one of two identical or similar persons." That meaning is how this author places Jesus and Thomas, an interpretation which helps solve certain little puzzles, as the reader will discover.

[14] Matthew, sometimes called 'Levi, Son of Alphaeus,' *Matthew* 9:9, 10:2&3, *Mark* 2:14&15, *Luke* 5:27-28. He authored the *Gospel of Matthew*, *Holy Bible*, Royal Publishers pp. 310, 817.

[15] Mary Magdalene is truly a puzzle. Some argue that she was the wife of Jesus, *Jesus and the Dead Sea Scrolls* and *The Messianic Legacy*, p.21. After he drove the evil spirits from her body, she remained with the group and followed Jesus until after his death. *Luke* 8:1-3, 24:10, *Mark* 15:42, *Matthew* 27:56, 61.

[16] John the Baptist is often included in the *Holy Bible*. He is sometimes depicted as an Essene (*What the Bible Really Says*, pp. 286-288). The reader should also see the many references in *The Dead Sea Scrolls and the Christian Myth*. *John* 1:19-34, *Luke* 1:5-25, 3:1-22, *Matthew* 3:1-17, *Mark* 1:1-11, *Smith's Bible Dictionary* pp. 315-16, "John the Baptist was of the priestly race by both parents" (Zacharias and Elizabeth).

[17] This strange myth can be found in three references: *Matthew* 4:1-11, *Mark* 1:12-13, and *Luke* 4:1-13.

[18] *Luke* 4:16-31.

Chapter 6: Jesus Heals and Teaches

[1] *Luke* 4:16-31.

[2] *Mark* 1:14-17, *Matthew* 5:19, 10:24-33, *Luke* 9:1-6.

[3] *Zachariah* 14:9, *Mark* 1:15.

[4] *Matthew* 7:24-29.

[5] *John* 2:12, *Matthew* 4:13-17.

[6] *Mark* 5:1-19, *Matthew* 8:28-34, *Luke* 8:26-40.

[7] *The Koran*, "Imrans." 3:47. "I come to confirm the Torah already revealed and make lawful to you some of the things you are forbidden..." (Jesus). Also, Matthew 5:17-20. "Think not that I am come to destroy the law, or the prophets: I am not come to destroy, but to fulfill."

[8] *Matthew* 21:12, *Luke* 13:15-16, *Mark* 2:27..

[9] *The Dead Sea Scrolls*, Allegro, p. 34. *The Columbia History of the World*, p. 418. Different people had different methods to measure time.

[10] *Matthew* 21:12, 25:27-29. Jesus advocated the sharing of the fruits of labor by the greater community, reasoning that God gave certain talents — abilities to produce value — to selected individuals which should be divided among those not so blessed. Therefore, money as a symbol of value could not be.

[11] *Matthew* 5:21-26. 'Brother' meant a person born of the same parents. The concept of brother as a common believer in the sect or comrade-in-arms came much later.

[12] *Matthew* 5:27-28. "...whosoever looketh on a woman to lust after her hath committed adultery with her already in his heart." No hidden meaning here!

[13] *Luke* 16:18, *Matthew* 5:27-32, *Mark* 10:11-12. The *Torah* allowed a husband to divorce without cause.Jesus commanded that the only grounds for divorce is adultery by the wife. "Whosoever putteth away his wife, and marrieth another, committeth adultery: and whosoever marrieth her that is put away from her husband committeth adultery."

[14] *Matthew* 5:33-37. "... But I say to you, Swear not at all; neither by heaven, for it is God's throne: Nor by earth...." Almost every public office and all military positions today require the recipient to swear or affirm loyalty to a government. No follower of Jesus may hold such offices.

[15] *Matthew* 5:38-48, 6:14-15.

[16] *Luke* 19:22-26, "Thou knowest that I was an austere man, taking up that I laid not down, and reaping that I did not sow: Where fore then gavest not thou my money into the bank..." *Thomas* 95, (Jesus said) "If you have money, do not lend it at interest. Rather, give it to someone from whom you will not get it back." *Luke* 7:41-43, *The Koran*, "The Cow." 2:272-282. *Torah* laws not changed by Jesus include *Exodus* 22:25, *Deuteronomy* 23:19-21.

[17] *Matthew* 22:37-39, *John* 13:34, *Corinthians* 13:13, *Luke* 6:27-36, *I John* 3:18.

[18] *Matthew* 6:2.

[19] *Matthew* 6:16-18, *Luke* 12:18-36.

[20] *Luke* 12:29-30, *Matthew* 6:25-34.

[21] *Luke* 12:13-21, "Take heed and be aware of covetousness; for a man's life consisteth not in the abundance of the things which he possesseth." A commercial business person could not enter holy places — *Thomas* 64: "Buyers and merchants will not enter the places of my father." Also *Thomas* 110: "Jesus said, 'Let someone who has found the world and has become wealthy renounce the world."

[22] *Matthew* 6:5-6. This is a very clear and direct prohibition against public prayer of any sort. It is unlawful for followers of Jesus to pray so others can hear them or even know they are praying. Examples of the private nature of prayer are found in *Matthew* 26:44, *Luke* 5:16, 20:46-47, 22:41, and *John* 14:16 and *Mark* 1:35, 6:46, 12:40 and 14:39.

[23] *Matthew* 6:12, 18:35. This was a general theme of the teaching of Jesus, but, as we shall see, he would teach vicious retribution against the enemy of the insurgency.

[24] *Matthew* 7:15-23.

[25] *Luke* 4:38-39, *Mark* 1:29-33, *Matthew* 8:14-17.

[26] *Luke* 4:40, *Mark* 1:34.

[27] *Mark* 1:40, *Luke* 5:12-15, *Matthew* 8:2-4.

[28] After the extended teaching at Capernaum, Jesus and his disciples never remained in one place for very long.

[29] *Luke* 10:1-24,. Clearly, Jesus intended these seventy to mix and mingle with the poor. The insurgents would need dependable cover, food and

supplies for the future operations. The seventy not only recruited, they were also an invaluable source of intelligence.

[30] *John* 2:1-12. Why Matthew, Mark and Luke did not also relate the lesson of this important event is unclear. Perhaps it is because the myth of feeding the five thousand is so similar.

[31] *Luke* 7:1-10. A centurion commanded a company of one hundred men, likely the size of the permanent garrison of men at Capernaum.

[32] *Matthew* 9:1-8, *Mark* 2:1-12, *Luke* 5:17-26.

[33] *Matthew* 9:10-13, *Luke* 5:30-39, *Mark* 2:15-17.

[34] *Matthew* 9:9, *Mark* 2:13-14, *Luke* 5:27-29.

[35] *Luke* 8:19-21, *Matthew* 12:46-50. Jesus had no time for family. The insurgency was all-important.

[36] *Mark* 6:32, *Matthew* 14:13-15, *John* 6:1-2.

[37] *Mark* 6:34.

[38] *Matthew* 14:15-21, Mark 6:33-44, *John* 6:5-14. The lesson of this little myth seems simple enough. However, many readers try to make the miracle much smaller by insisting that Jesus actually expanded the food quantity.

[39] *Matthew* 14:22-32, *Mark* 6:45-52, *John* 6:16-21. As recorded, this story makes little sense. Certainly, the reporters—none of them sailors—viewed the event as extraordinary. Here is an explanation of what might have happened.

[40] *Mark* 4:35-41, *John* 6:22-25, *Matthew* 14:23-27. *Mark* tells the story best.

[41] *Mark* 6:33-56, *Matthew* 14:34-36.

[42] *Matthew* 15:1-20, *Mark* 7:18-23.

[43] *Matthew* 8:28-34. This myth explains why the meat of hogs should not be consumed by any followers of Jesus. With this act, Jesus reaffirmed Jewish law.

[44] *Luke* 8:41-56, *Matthew* 9:18-26, *Mark* 5:21-43.

[45] *Mark* 9:1-13, *Matthew* 17:1-13, *Luke* 9:28-36.

[46] *Matthew* 5:17. "Do not think that I came to destroy the Law or the Prophets. I did not come to destroy but to fulfill."

John 1:17 "For the law was given through Moses, but grace and truth came through Jesus Christ."

The Koran, "Battle Array." 61:1. "...(Jesus said) I am sent forth to you from God to confirm the Torah..."

Any law from the Old Testament that Jesus did not specifically change remained.

[47] *Matthew* Chapter 5. This paragraph is a summary of topics covered earlier in this chapter. Chapter 5 is a concise outline of the social philosophy of Jesus.

[48] *Matthew* 22:15-22, *Mark* 12:13-17, *Luke* 20:20-26, *Thomas* 100. Jesus specifically allowed the paying of taxes to Rome with Roman money. He neither condemned nor sanctioned tithes in the form of money engraved with Caesar's image but inferred that coveting such symbols was blasphemy.

[49] *Matthew* 12:46-50, 10:37, *Mark* 3:31-35, 7:11-13, *Luke* 8:19-21, 20:35. "But they which shall be accounted worthy to obtain that world, and the resurrection from the dead, neither marry, nor are given in marriage."

Thomas 105, "Whoever knows the father and the mother will be called the child of a whore."

Jesus: A Life, A. N. Wilson, p.120. "His (Jesus') recorded utterances about the family as an institution are all hostile to it."

Mark 7:12 "And ye suffer him no more to do aught for his father or his mother."

Luke 14:26 "If any man come to me, and hate not his father, and mother, and wife, and children, and brethren, and sisters, yea, and his own life also, he cannot be my disciple."

In *Luke* 8:19-21, Jesus refused to see his mother, brothers and sisters. Jesus' disdain for the family unit is strong evidence that he may have been of the Essene sect.

Chapter 7: The Conspiracy Widens

[1] *Matthew* 15:21, *Mark* 7:24-30. I speculate that Matthew and Mark did not personally *admit* who made the trip, "Then Jesus went thence, and departed into the coasts of Tyre and Sidon."

See also *Matthew* 15:29. Almost in the same breath as he told of the trip to Tyre, Matthew tells of Jesus departing south along the Sea of Galilee.

[2] With only one healing and no recorded preaching incidents in this myth, one would suspect a more practical purpose for the trip. Simon of Cyrene and products of Cyrene show up later in our story.

[3] *Matthew* 15:22-28.

[4] Mary Magdalene has mystified readers and inspired painters for centuries. Some say she married Jesus at Cana and they produced three children (*Holy Blood, Holy Grail*). Some say she was a common whore. She and other women gave some "substance" to Jesus, according to Luke. Was that substance sex? Was she a disciple of the same rank as the twelve men or did she follow Jesus and the group as a beggar? She was a loyal follower. See *Matthew* 27:55-61, *Luke* 8:2-3, *Mark* 16:1-9, *John* 20:1-2, 20:11-18.

[5] *Luke* 8:3.

[6] Manna is found miraculously supplied by God to those in need. See *John* 6:31, *Exodus* 16:4 and 15, and *Deuteronomy* 8:3.

[7] *Matthew* 10:34-39. "think not that I am come to send peace on earth: I come not to send peace but a sword."

Luke 12:49-59. "For from henceforth there shall be five in one house divided, three against two, and two against three."

Thomas 16. "...I have come to impose conflicts upon the earth: fire, sword, war."

[8] One modern historian argues that Joseph of Arimathea was a rich shipping trader who took Jesus by ship to what would become England.

"Medieval tradition portrays Joseph of Arimathea as a custodian of the Holy Grail." *Holy Flood*, p. 357.

[9] *Acts* 12:12&25 identify the home of John Mark. Acts 20:9-12 portrays John Mark still as a young man during the preaching days of Paul when he dies and recovers. *Jesus and the Riddle of the Dead Sea Scrolls*, Thiering, pp. 81-82, identifies "John Mark Eutychus" as "Bartholomew" and the author of the *Gospel of John*.

Jesus, Crossan, pp. 186-90, discusses John Mark. *John* 20:2 contains "...the other disciple, whom Jesus loved." See also *The Passover Plot*, Schonfield, P. 100, 103, 105.

Author's note: No other disciple was given the very intimate title, "Beloved." It is and often was the title often given a wife. John Mark was very young. He, as we shall see, showed deep love for Jesus. It is not unreasonable to place the relationship as one not uncommon in Greek culture between an older, richer and educated man and a younger man. John Mark later worked with Paul and perhaps wrote *Mark*. John did identify himself as the author of *John* 21:20&24, "...the disciple whom Jesus loved..." and "This is the disciple which testifieth of these things...," *Bible Handbook*, Henry Halley, 22nd Edition, Halley, 1959, p.484.

[10] Nicodemus purportedly wrote the rather long 'Gospel of Nicodemus' now printed in *The Lost Books*.He was a Pharisee (*John* 3:1-12) and testified for Jesus at the trial of Jesus (*John* 7:50-52). See also *Jesus*, Crossan, pp. 157-59.

[11] This is the basis for all religion. Religion must be accepted on faith, not reason. The myth of Adam and Eve and the fruit of knowledge illustrates to the faithful that man should not seek knowledge. Man should accept only the word of God, who knows and understands all.

Genesis 3:6&7 says "...and a tree to be desired to make one wise" was forbidden. *Mark* 10:15 "Whosoever shall not receive the kingdom of God as a little child, he shall not enter therein." A child is presumed to be without the ability to reason.

[12] *John* 3:13. "And no man hath ascended up to heaven but that he came down from heaven, even the Son of Man which is in heaven." This, combined with Jesus' statement that only saints were in heaven and man could live forever on earth but not in heaven, contradicts beliefs held by most Christians today.

[13] *John* 2:13-25. Only John tells of this angry incident in the Temple.

[14] *Luke* 16:20-25.

[15] *Luke* 16:24. This shows another clear example of ancestor worship by Jesus. Abraham is the "father" and ruler of Heaven.

[16] *II Kings* 17:24-41.

[17] *Genesis* Chapter 46.

[18] *John* 4:1-42.

[19] *Matthew* 16:13-20. Matthew does not mention any contact with the people on this unexplained trip. Apparently, Jesus was hiding under the nose of the Roman governor-general and the largest military garrison in the area.

Chapter 8: WAR

[1] *John* 11:6. "When he had heard therefore that he was sick, he abode two days still in the same place where he was."

[2] *John* 11:1-46, the only place this story is told.

[3] *John* 11:47-57. These verses relate the reaction of the council to the Lazarus miracle.

[4] *John* 11:54. The Ephraim were one of the largest and most important tribes of the twelve.

[5] The group included John Mark and Mary Magdalene.

[6] *Luke* 17:20-37, *Matthew* 24:6-28, *Mark* 13:1-23. The war Jesus forecast would come to fruition thirty years later. It resulted in a Roman victory over a despoiled land.

[7] For a satirical view of James read *The Bad News Bible* by David Voss.

[8] Abraham is "he who commands me."

[9] Wanderings, Chaim Potok, Fawcett, 1978. pp284-287. "...the Latin word sica means curved dagger..." Successful terrorism demands either a passive or friendly populace.

[10] Holy Blood, Holy Grail, Baigent, Leigh,& Lincoln, pp350-352. *Matthew* 27:16-26. *Mark* 15:7. "And there was one named Barabbas, which lay bound with them that had made insurrection with him, who had committed murder in the insurrection." The Death of Jesus, Carmichael, p.146.

Chapter 9: War Fellowship

[1] *John* 19:23. "......and also his coat: now the coat was without seam, woven from top throughout." The unique technique used to make this garment was considered significant by the author of John. If that art were known today it would surely be so time-consuming as to be impractical.

[2] *Luke* 17:11-19. Ephraim seems to have been a sort of command center. The presence of so many lepers indicates it was a place to consign the sick and dying. An abundance of government officials were unlikely in such a place.

[3] An attempt by Luke to show the 'Jews' did not accept Jesus. The Jews were the authorities in power, not the general population.

[4] *Matthew* 19:16-30, *Mark* 10:17-31, *Luke* 18:18-30.

[5] An example of Jesus' quick temper. *Luke* 18:25, *Mark* 10:25.

[6] *Matthew* 20:1-16.

[7] There seems to be no open preaching from Ephraim until the triumphant entry into Jerusalem.

[8] Of course there is little mention in the accounts of the disciples about details of the insurgency. To write down such details would betray the principles of insurgency and common sense. See my 'Introduction' for a discussion of security within an insurgency organization.

[9]*Matthew* 21:2-7, *Mark* 11:2-7, *Luke* 19:30-34. These three accounts are so similar that they must be either plagiarism or written by the same author.

[10]*Matthew* 26:17-19, *Luke* 22:7-13.

[11]The most common drug ingested by Israelites was most likely mandrake. Smith's *Bible Dictionary* notes "Dr. Richardson ('Lectures on Alcohol,' 1881) tried some experiments with wine made of the root of mandrake, and found it narcotic, causing sleep, so that the ancients used it as an anaesthetic." Hugh Schonfield, *The Passover Plot* p.167 comments on the drug Jesus drank on the cross: "If what he received had been the normal wine vinegar diluted with water the effect would have been stimulating. In this case it was exactly the opposite. Jesus lapsed quickly into complete unconsciousness. His body sagged. His head rolled on his breast, and to all intents and purposes he was a dead man."

[12]*John* 13:36-38, *Luke* 22:31-34, *Matthew* 26:31-35. These narrators could never admit these events were planned. So we see the plot presented as some kind of sinister prophesy.

[13]*John* 13:21-30. *Luke* 22:21-23. *Mark* 14:18-21. *Matthew* 26:21-25.

[14]*Luke* 13:4, *Matthew* 27:16, *Mark* 15:7. Matthew describes Barabbas as a 'notable' prisoner. This indicates he was considered an important man. Of Barabbas, Mark says "...who had committed murder in the insurrection."

[15]*Matthew* 23:1-39. This last sermon is a rousing call to arms. It identifies the enemy as evil and predicts victory for the good.

[16]*Matthew* 21:8-11, *Luke* 19:35-40, *John* 12:12-18, *Mark* 11:7-11.

[17]*Mark* 11:15-19, *Luke* 19:45-48, *Matthew* 21:10-16. The time spent in the temple could have been days or weeks as suggested by *Luke* 19:47, "And he taught daily in the temple...", or a much shorter time. Here I suggest that it does not make sense that Jesus could have entered as the clear proclaimed 'King' and enjoyed a leisurely period of days or weeks of open teaching without being arrested for sedition.

[18]Psalm 89

[19]Psalm 72.

[20]Psalm 58.

Chapter 10: Death of Jesus

[1] *The Passover Plot*, Schonfield, p.166. Schonfield attributes the tomb and garden location to ancient historian Josephus. Schonfield also refers to Apostle Bartholomew's *The Book of Resurrection* for hints the gardener (named Philogenes) might have been upset that Jesus' vault was in his field (Schonfield p. 171). Schofield refers to a document by E. A. Willis Budge, Oriental Manuscript #6804 at the British Museum. *John 18:1* locates the garden near a brook called Cedron. *Matthew* 26:36 and *Mark* 14:32 name the garden Gethsemane.

[2] *Matthew* 26:14-16, *Mark* 14:10-11, *Luke* 22:2-6. The bribe, thirty pieces of silver, is borrowed from Zachariah 11:12. "...So they weighed my price, thirty pieces of silver."

[3] Pilate had good reason to worry. The handling of the Davidians was not looked upon with favor by Rome. Within one year, Pontius was on trial and Herod fired.

[4] Abraham was the father of Israel and the Kingdom of David. Jesus prays to his father, not God. *John* 17:1-26.

[5] Latter day revisionists dropped the word cohort to make it appear much less a military encounter. The Spanish language Bibles retain the more descriptive term. *Sagrada Bíblia*, Bíblioteca de Áutores Crístianos, Madríd, 1985, San Juan 18:3: "Judas, pués, tománd la cohorte ý los álguaciles de los póntifices y friseos, von allí con linternas, ý hachas, ý armas. "As now published, the synoptic Gospels still strongly suggest a military confrontation.

John 18:3, A band of men "...cometh thither with lanterns and torches and weapons."

Mark 14:43, "...with him a great multitude with swords and staves..."

Luke 22:49, "...shall we smite with the sword?"

Matthew 26:47, "...and with him a great multitude with swords and staves...." *Stave* is a type of spear.

[6] *The Passover Plot*, Schonfield, pp. 152-3.

[7] *John* 11:47-57.

[8] *The Death of Jesus*, Carmichael, P. 38-39. *The Messianic Legacy*, Baigent, Leigh and Lincoln, p. 72.

[9] Jesus rescued one woman from death by stoning. He did not change the law.

[10] *Luke* 23:26, *Matthew* 27:32. Simon of Cyrene carries the cross behind (after) Jesus. Only Luke and Matthew mention Simon of Cyrene. Other authors might have thought mention of a foreigner would have been too dangerous.

[11] The priests wanted to change the sign to identify Jesus as 'He who would be King of the Jews.' Pilate refused.

[12] *The Lost Books*, Infancy 8:7. "And these two thieves shall be with me at the same time upon the cross, Titus on my right hand, and Dumachus on my left......"

[13]'Mary' was a title often given to Zealot revolutionaries. 'Mary' indicates unyielding persistence. A strong minded woman with unyielding opinions and fixed purpose. So many Marys in the Bible make for much confusion.

[14] Jesus was now naked upon the cross.

[15] *John* 19:24. John quotes *Psalm* 22:18.

[16] *Mark* 15:20-41, *Matthew* 27:33-54, *Luke* 23:44-46, *John* 19:18-27, *Psalm* 22.

Glossary

Abraham: Mythological father of all racial Jews and founder of the religion of the single God, YHWH.

Andrew: Brother of Simon Peter. Follower of John the Baptist and later, Jesus.

Anna: Mother of Holy Mary. Aristocratic descendent of King David. Wife of Joachim.

Annas: A Sadducee scribe from Galilee. Became a priest of Temple Jerusalem at age 30. Encouraged the conviction of Jesus for sedition.

Apocrypha: Writings rejected for content that is damaging to one's own notions.

Archelaus, Herod: Ruler of Judea.

Asher: One of the tribes in Holy Mary's family tree.

Barabbas: Led riot against Roman troops.

Bartholomew, Nathanael: Of noble birth through the Talmai family of Galilee. Life-long follower of Jesus and the insurgency.

Bethlehem: Small town to the south of Jerusalem. Spiritual home of the Kingdom of David.

Caiaphas: High Priest and chief judge of religious law during the trial of Jesus.

Christ: Greek word for the Promised ruler or Messiah.

Dumachus: A highway robber. Executed same day as Jesus.

Elizabeth: Cousin of Holy Mary. Mother of John the Baptist. Wife of Zacharias.

Essene: A sect that worshipped the single God of Abraham.

Father: Usually referred to a deified Abraham as progenitor worshipped as God.

Gabriel: An angel that visited both Anna and Holy Mary in the form of a man the night each conceived.

Herod Antipas: Ruler/administrator of Galilee.

Herod Archelaus: Son of Herod the Great. Ruled Israel and Judea at the pleasure of Rome at the time of Jesus' birth.

Herod the Great: Father of ruling family of all the region that included Israel, Judea, and Galilee.

Insurgency: A pre-planned process by which widespread popular discontent aids a small group of rebels to overthrow the government.

Insurgent: *adj.* Rising in revolt against civil authority or a government in power; rebellious. *—n.* A member of a political party who rebels against its leadership.

Israelite: Any member of the twelve tribes of Abraham.

James Boanorges: Son of Mary and Zebedee. Abandoned by Salomé and Zebedee to be raised by Cleophas of Nazareth.

James the Younger: Half-brother of Jesus and a member of the insurgency. Son of Joseph and his first wife, Mary.

Jesse: Father of King David. Progenitor of Jesus.

Jesus Messiah: Pretender to the throne of King David. Claimed royal and priestly pedigree. After death, he was worshipped as a God.

Joachim: Father of Holy Mary. Husband of Anna. Claimed to be dynastic successor of the priest, Aaron.

John the Baptist: Famous preacher who changed the ritual of Essene baptism. Cousin of Jesus.

John Boanorges: Brother of James Boanorges. Disciple of Jesus.

John Mark Eutychus: Rich young Essene, lover of Jesus, who lived in a large home in Bethany. He took the name Lazarus after accepting the philosophy of Jesus. His father owned a house in Jerusalem.

Joseph: Selected by the priests of Qumran to be husband of Holy Mary. Claimed Davidian lineage. Husband of two Mary's.

Joseph of Arimathea: Trader and influential member of the ruling council. Secret insurgent.

Judas Iscariot: One of twelve lieutenants of Jesus. Saved from death by Jesus when both were young boys. Deeply involved with execution schemes.

Judeah: Ancient member of the Asher tribe. Progenitor of Joseph, father of Jesus.

Judas Thaddeus: (Jude): Half brother of Jesus by Joseph and his first wife named Mary. Raised as a brother of Jesus. Fury Zealot.

Judith: Anna's personal handmaid/slave.

Lazarus: See John Mark Eutychus.

Malcus: Captain of a Roman cohort. Egyptian by birth.

Mandrake: A common drug used during biblical times.

Martha: Sister of Mary of Bethany and John Mark 'Lazarus.'

Mary: The title given a female that is strong, independent, stubborn and sure-willed.

Mary of Bethany: Sister of John Mark 'Lazarus.'

Mary, Holy: Mother of Jesus and Thomas. Daughter of Anna and Joachim. Raised and educated by apocalyptical priests at Qumran monastery. Second wife of Joseph (both wives were called 'Mary').

Mary: First wife of Joseph. Forced to leave Joseph to become surrogate mother of two of Zebedee and Salome's children, John and James.

Nary Magdalene: Became disciple of Jesus after he cured her of the seven demons.

Matthew Levi: Minor government official who became a follower of Jesus and the cause.

Messiah: Word for the promised ruler of the Kingdom of David.

Nation, Jewish: A diverse group descending from twelve tribes held together by their common worship of the single God of Abraham.

Nicodemus: Member of Sanhedrin ruling council. Underground insurgent.

Pantera: Roman soldier.Friend of Holy Mary. Rumored by some who did not believe Jesus' divinity to be the father of Jesus and Thomas.

Petroius: Centurion commander of about one hundred man Roman military unit in Capernaum. Converted to the faith of Abraham. Detailed to guard the tomb of Jesus.

Pharisee: Pious religious sect that worshipped the single God of Abraham.

Philip: Friend of Andrew and Simon Peter. Member of the insurgency.

Pontius Pilate: Roman governor-general of Palestine appointed by Caesar. Headquartered in Caesarea.

Qumran: Principal monastery of the Essene sect.

Righteous Teacher: Savior anticipated by the Essene sect.

Sadducees: A religious sect that worshipped the single God of Abraham. Produced a high number of priests and therefore controlled the administration of the law.

Salem: A dyer by trade.

Salomé, Herod: Daughter of Herod the Great. Minor ruler. Had John the Baptist executed.

Sanhedrin: Supreme council of priestly authority. Interpreted and enforced all Israelite law.

Silphium laciniatum: A drug grown and processed in Cyrene.

Simon of Cyrene: Trader and broker of drugs. Carried cross for Jesus.

Simon Magus: Rival magician to Jesus.

Simon Peter: A commercial fisherman. Early follower of Jesus.

Simon Zelote: Military leader of the insurgency.

Son of God: Any male Essene faithful.

Thomas: Full brother of Jesus. Son of Holy Mary and Joseph.

Titus: A highway robber.

True Purple: Made from secret Tyrean dye. Denotes divine authority. Worn by Jesus.

YHWH: Name of God of Abraham spoken only by priests.

Zaccheus: Greek tutor of Jesus.

Zacharias: Husband of Elizabeth. High priest of Qumran. Murdered by Herod the Great.

Zealots: Militant insurgents.

Zebedee: Husband of Salomé Herod. Father of John Boanorges by Joseph's first wife, Mary.

Zeinunus: A young friend of the boy Jesus. Fell from a roof and died.

Dogma

Book of Mormon.
The Church of Jesus Christ of-Latter Day Saints. First translated and published in 1830.

Book of J.
Translated by David Rosenberg. New York: Weidenfeld, 1990.

Columbia History of the World.
Edited by John Garraty & Peter Gay. New York: Harper, 1972.

Gospel of Thomas.
New translation by Marvin Meyer. San Francisco: Harper: 1992.

Holy Bible.
Royal Publishers, Nashville, 1966.

Koran.
Translated by N. J. Dawood. New York: Penguin: 1990.

Lost Books of the Bible.
Reprint of World Publishing 1926 edition. New Jersey: Gramercy, 1979.

Sagrada Bíblia.
Salamanca University edition. Bíblioteca de Áutores Crístianos, Madríd, 1985.

Bibliography

Allegro, John M. *The Dead Sea Scrolls and the Christian Myth.* Prometheus Books, New York, 1984.

Baigent, Leigh & Lincoln. *Holy Blood, Holy Grail.* New York: Dell, 1983.

Baigent, Leigh & Lincoln. *The Messianic Legacy.* New York: Dell, 1989.

Ballon, Robert. *The Other Jesus.* New York: Doubleday, 1972.

Manfred, Barthel. *What the Bible Really Says.* Quill, New York, 1983.

Bishop, Jim. *The Day Christ Was Born & The Day Christ Died.* New York: Galahad, 1993.

Carmichael, Joel. *The Death of Jesus.* Horizon, New York, 1982.

Charlesworth, James (editor). *Jesus and the Dead Sea Scrolls.* New York: Doubleday, 1993.

Cohen, A. *Everyone's Talmud.* New York: Schocken Books, 1975.

Crossan, John Dominic. *Jesus: A Revolutionary.* Harper, San Francisco, 1989.

D'Ancona, Matthew and Carsten Peter Thiede. *Eyewitness to Jesus: Amazing New Evidence About the Origin of the Gospels.* New York: Doubleday, 1997.

Deen, Edith. *All The Women of The Bible.* New York: Harper, 1955.

Dimont, Max. *Appointment in Jerusalem.* New York: St. Martin's Press, 1991.

Farmer, William. *Maccabees, Zealots and Josephus.* New York: Columbia University, 1956.

Graae, Johan. *A Review of Bible Critique*. New York: Vantage Press, 1993.

Grant, Michael. *Jesus: An Historian's Review of the Gospels*. New York: MacMillan, 1992.

Grossen, John D. Jesus: *A Revolutionary Biography*. San Francisco: Harper, 1995.

Hally, Henry. *Bible Handbook*. Chicago: Hally, 1959 (22nd Edition).

Joseph, Gardner (editor). *Atlas of The Bible*. Pleasantville, New York: Reader's Digest, 1981.

Kaari, Ward (editor). *Jesus and His Times*. Pleasantville, New York: Reader's Digest, 1988.

McKinsey, Dennis. *The Encyclopedia of Biblical Errancy*. Amherst, New York: Prometheus, 1955.

Nelson, Thomas. *Bible Handbook*. Nashville, Tennessee: Nelson Publishers, 1993.

Pike, Albert. *Morals and Dogma*. Charleston, 1871 (Richmond: Jenkins, 1921 edition).

Potok, Chaim. *Wanderings*. New York: Fawcett, 1988.

Sacchi, Paolo. *Recovering Jesus' Formative Background*. Doubleday, 1992.

Schonfield, Hugh Joseph. *The Jesus Party*. New York: MacMillan, 1974.

Schonfield, Hugh Joseph. *The Passover Plot*. Rockport, MA: Element, 1994.

Shanks, Herschel. *Understanding the Dead Sea Scrolls*. New York: Random House, 1992.

Smith, Norton. *Jesus the Magician*. Barnes & Noble: New York, 1993.

Smith, William. *A Dictionary of the Bible* (Revised and Edited by F. N. and M.A. Piloubet). Nashvilee: Thomas Nelson Publishers, 1986.

Stalker, Rev. James, Eaton and Mains. *The Ethics of Jesus*. New York, 1909.

Thiering, Barbara. *Jesus and the Riddle of the Dead Sea Scrolls*. Harper, San Francisco, 1988.

Voss, David. *The Bad News Bible: The New Testament*. Amherst, NY: Prometheus, 1995.

Whiston, William (translator). *Complete Works of Josephus*. Grand Rapids, MI: Kregel Publications, 1991.

Wilson, A. N. *Jesus: A Life*. Norton, New York, 1992.